*Don't Bother
to Come in
on Monday*

Don't Bother to Come in on Monday

What To Do When You Lose Your Job

BARBARA HOWELL

St. Martin's Press   New York

TO BILLY

Library of Congress No. 72 –91372
Manufactured in the United States of America.
No part of this book may be reproduced without
permission in writing from the publisher.

St. Martin's Press
175 Fifth Avenue
New York, N.Y., 10010

AFFILIATED PUBLISHERS: Macmillan & Company, Limited, London
—also at Bombay, Calcutta, Madras and Melbourne—
the Macmillan Company of Canada, Limited, Toronto

Contents

Acknowledgments

Most of the names used in this book are fictitious. For obvious professional reasons, the people who were fired preferred to have some kind of alias, whereas some of the employment agents and psychologists withheld the use of their names out of concern for their clients and patients about whom they had revealed so much.

To all the people who helped me with this book, whether identified or not, I give my sincerest thanks.

Introduction

Dr. William Traynor, a New York economist, was afraid he was going to be fired. At least twice a week, he was visited by the same nightmare.

"There is this cocktail party in a magnificent Fifth Avenue apartment, completely covered in white, wall-to-wall carpeting. Everyone is very polite. But I know it is my last cocktail party. At one point, the hostess comes over and says, 'O.K., let's go.'

"She brings me into a room that has pictures all over the walls. But there is one blank spot on the wall, and I know it is for me. She says, 'Please stand over there.' And I say, 'But there will be blood all over the floor.' Because I know then that I am going to be shot."

A travel agent from Philadelphia says firing to her is "like capital punishment. Your company is the jury that decides you should be eliminated from the human race . . . and you can't call a cop."

"To be cut off from your job is a kind of castration," a teacher in the Los Angeles public school system explained breezily.

The subject of firing is so often surrounded in mystery and fear. The word firing—as well as its synonyms: axed, sacked, canned—is charged with violence. Although many concede that some individuals can benefit from dismissal, all are unanimous in never wanting it to happen to them.

Yet there is practically no employee living today who has not, at one time or another, considered the possibility of being fired. And with our recessions, dying industries, and mergers, most people have a good chance of being politely told, "Don't bother to come in on Monday," at least once in a lifetime.

The purpose of this book is to bring the whole subject of firing out into the open and explore it from every angle.

To obtain as much information as possible, I have spoken to personnel agents, employees and employers—from clerks to presidents of large corporations—psychiatrists, and even one astrologist for their direct accounts of the firing experience. Their stories, theories, statements, and advice are the substance of this book.

My research started in 1970, possibly the lowest point of the recession. During that period, *Fortune* magazine estimated that executive unemployment may have climbed as high as 15 percent. No one knows for sure how many people were out of work—or shaking with fear that they might soon be. Statistics on white-collar unemployment, especially at the middle-management and executive levels, are not kept by any federal agency. However, executive recruiters told *Fortune* that the volume of unsolicited résumés crossing their desks had tripled, sometimes even quadrupled, in that year.

The time seemed ripe to investigate the lives and thoughts of all those men and women out on the street. So for two years, that's what I did.

From the words and experiences of the people I interviewed, the fact that getting fired need not be a major disaster became increasingly evident. While it may cause some self-destructive behavior and contain much anguish, crazy joys, and tremendous challenge, it is not like castration, capital punishment, or facing a firing squad. For most people, it is simply one step on the road from one job to another.

BARBARA HOWELL
EAST HAMPTON, N.Y. 1972

Chapter I

THE EXIT INTERVIEW

When the Cosa Nostra wants to fire a man, they're very direct about it. They pump him full of bullets and dump him into the nearest river. In the earlier years of the English monarchy, the weak and inefficient were often poisoned, beheaded, or kicked upstairs to the Tower of London.

In the corporate state, dismissal is far gentler—so gentle that some people don't even know they're being fired.

R. F., the chairman of a huge international chemical corporation, was bored and alcoholic. To spice up his days, he indulged in wildcat schemes that invariably resulted in his buying too high and selling too low. Firing him or retiring him would have been a long, tough struggle. He controlled 20 percent of the corporation stock.

Before R.F. was able to run the business into bankruptcy, a member of the board, who personally knew the President of the United States, had a brilliant idea: "Let's get R. F. made an ambassador."

The request was granted. R. F. sailed off to one of Europe's largest capitals, chuckling over the thought that he had been chosen for the post because of his fine record at the chemical corporation.

R. F.'s case is not as uncommon as one would think. The *Wall Street Journal* reports that this practice, called "dehiring" or "outplacing," is taking hold in many companies and has reached the middle-management level.

Corporations actually hire recruiting firms to find jobs for unwanted employees. When the employee "quits" to go to his new position, he has no idea that his own company paid the recruiter to lure him away.

Murder and dehiring are the two extremes of the firing procedure. In both cases, the individual is helpless to do anything about the firing. He is either dead or blissfully unaware that he has been canned—and he doesn't need to do anything.

But in that vast middle ground where the average firing occurs, there are several opportunities for the victim to alter the course of his firing and make his presence felt.

"When a person's being fired, he should never just sit there like a rejected executive plaything. If there's anything he can do to make his situation better, he should do it," says a formerly fired accountant.

Depending on who is doing the severing and why, a person can obtain for himself any number of benefits ranging from extra money to getting the job back—*during the firing interview itself*. Not in all cases—but in enough to make them worth mentioning.

Management's Feelings About Firing

For the employee to understand how the exit interview can be manipulated to his advantage, he must first realize that most employers hate to fire. Before and during the act, they are in a tense, almost guilt-ridden state.

"I always feel like hell about firing someone," says an executive of a large soup company. "Ordinarily I have to have two drinks at lunch to fortify myself for the ordeal. Hell, I know I'm much more miserable than the guy I'm kicking out."

The vice-president of a car-rental firm, who has fired at least twenty people in his lifetime, confessed that he keeps the nameplates of all the people he has ever fired in a small cupboard at home. The night before he must fire a subordinate, he hauls out his stack of nameplates. "I just count them, think of the people's faces, stack them up, you know. Just to remind myself that I can be hardboiled and I'm not a patsy. The next day, terminating the guy is a little easier."

Others claim that they have lost hours of sleep before a single firing, taken up smoking again, or hated themselves for days afterward.

Several executives lamented that no book or study on firing had been written from *their* point of view.

"Unlike hiring, there is no well-developed science of dismissal," complains a New York business administrator. "We have elaborate procedures for hiring and testing—like evaluation and salary scales. But for firing, there is no comparable organization or structure or code of ethics." Like so many people confronted with shaky moral and economic decisions, he dreams of a scientific theory to bail him out.

Overseas, the problem of firing is less troublesome for management. In most European countries, the government has stepped in with laws and compensation regulations that control the firing process and relieve employers of much of their uncertainties. In Japan, there is no firing, just job relocation or adjustment.

Here in America, the government's approach to white-collar firing is strictly laissez-faire. While this is more of a problem to the subordinate than to the superior, that doesn't mean that some members of management aren't greatly disturbed by their freedom to fire. They are so disturbed, in fact, that the employee is not half as powerless as he may think he is.

Bargaining for Severance

A senior executive for a large cosmetics firm who has been on the losing side of the firing situation only once, recommended, "The minute the words 'We really regret this but . . .' are out of the boss's mouth, you should leap in and start bargaining for more severance pay. Because that's when the boss is at his weakest. If you apply just a little pressure, maybe you can up the severance by 50 percent.

If you're in a position to write a juicy little memo that could jeopardize the boss's career, by all means allude to that fact. Subtly. It should never look like blackmail. But you've got to do it right away. Once you've left the building and word's out that you've been dumped, you're less of a threat.''

Howard Bigley, a young assistant salesmanager for a small mid-western manufacturing firm, did just that. For two years, his boss, a rotund, easygoing sales manager, had been involved with several outside interests and had neglected his supervisory duties. Howard, who was overqualified for his job anyhow, amused himself by grabbing the spotlight away from his superior and making himself the nerve center of the sales division. The board of directors and customers quickly caught on to the situation and requested Howard's electric presence during almost all negotiations. One day his boss woke up.

Shortly thereafter, he called Howard in and drawled, ''There isn't room in this corporation for both of us. There are two solutions to the problem. One is that I quit and find a new job. The other is that I fire you. I've been looking for a job for two months and didn't find one. So I'm firing you.''

''He must have really planned that speech carefully,'' Howard mused. ''It was the old territorial-imperative, get-out-of-town approach. But I had enough presence of mind to remind him *why* I had been able to usurp his power by asking him how his extra-office affairs were going. Then I demanded six months' severance. I got four. But that was better than the two weeks he traditionally gave people.''

Howard felt absolutely no moral compunction about the way he got his extra severance. ''High-level executives who are retired early are given a larger pension if they sign a contract promising not to work for a competitor. If they're allowed to indulge in that kind of gentlemanly blackmail, why shouldn't others, too?''

''I think any kind of blackmail is uncalled for,'' an editor for a textbook publishing house protested. ''But it is possible to extend your severance if you haven't been warned. I mean, if they just fire you without any advance notice, a man could say something like, 'Why this is *unconscionable* to dismiss me without any warning—I have five children,' and so on. Of course that only works if the boss really hasn't given any previous warning—or thinks his warnings didn't sink in.''

"If you have suffered any kind of physical disability from a job, never forget to bring it up when they are firing you,'' says an agent for a monolithic talent agency. "When they told me they were going to let me go, I reminded them of the nervous breakdown I'd had three years before while on the job. Extra compensation for it showed up in my last paycheck.''

Becoming a Consultant

After five years of dedicated hard work, banker Paul Weintraub got control of a small stodgy Pennsylvania bank and began turning it into a progressive, growing enterprise. When the time came to dispose of its venerable but ultraconservative sixty-five-year-old president, Weintraub found the experience very upsetting.

"Old Mr. Lancaster looked so downcast, so wounded, I realized that I couldn't do as I planned and fire him outright. So I asked him to come in once a week as a consultant for the rest of his life," confessed Mr. Weintraub.

Who knows if Mr. Lancaster's tragic demeanor was genuine or a superb acting performance? It worked. He got more than Weintraub had previously been willing to give.

Staying on as a consultant can be a solid, income-producing activity while going about the business of finding a new job. If Mr. Lancaster's tactics seem a little too melodramatic, there are other ways to go about obtaining consultant work.

One is for the employee to mention his intimate relationships with clients and claim that there will be a strong reaction if he abruptly disappears.

If a person has been maintaining a fairly complicated filing system, he might remark that no one but himself will ever be able to decipher it, and amiably add, "unless I come in once a week to explain its intricacies to my successor."

One disadvantage to bargaining for money or consultant work is that the employee must bow quickly to fate and get down to the business of negotiating his payoff right away, thus eliminating the possibility of trying to convince the boss *not* to fire him.

Bullying Your Way Back In

When Charles Stevenson, a muscular, extroverted insurance salesman, was called into his boss's office and the boss started elaborating on Charles's poor performance, Charles roared, "Are you *firing ME?*" His superior sat and listened while Charles pounded on the desk and bitterly complained that he had been given no time to display his true worth, had been robbed of real opportunities, etc., etc.

The stupefied boss completely backed down and protested that he was only trying to *warn* Charles. Charles stayed on the payroll for three more months while he hunted for a new job.

He didn't get any severance, but, as he said, "It's a lot easier to find a job when you already have one. It was worth putting a little pressure on my boss to let me stay."

Debating Your Way Back In

Another way to fight a firing is to engage the boss in a cool, factual debate.

A retail buyer talked her way out of being sacked when a superior two rungs above her was delegated to fire her. Since he barely knew her personally, he had jotted down a brief list of all her faults on a piece of paper. He referred to it frequently as he rattled off the reasons for her discharge from the department store. Why he did the firing and not her immediate superior was a question she couldn't answer. But she decided to take advantage of the distance between them and his ignorance of her day-to-day activities.

After he had finished telling her how and when she had been inadequate, she looked at him bug-eyed and said, "Would you repeat that please?"

Taking a deep breath, he went through the whole rigmarole again. "It gave me time to prepare my defense, you see. After he finished, I rebutted each accusation point by point—most of them were actually unfair—and gave him a logical, reasonable excuse or explanation for every infraction he mentioned. It worked. I stayed on for six months until I found a job in another store.

If it had been her immediate superior who had fired her, would she have been able to talk him out of it? "I don't know. He really disliked me. He was furious when I told him that I had not been fired and was being given another chance."

The Yippee-I'm-Fired Ploy

Larry Kranz, a junior executive with an Ohio steel company, took a decidedly more positive approach to his near-firing. When his boss said he was going to have to let him go, Larry said, "That's just great. I'm prepared for it because I have the strongest, toughest résumé of any guy on the job market. I'm *delighted* to look for a new job."

Résumé? Delighted? The boss was understandably curious about Larry's reaction. He asked to se the résumé which, beautifully worded, listed all of Larry's major accomplishments—seen from Larry's highly original point of view.

The boss was so impressed (and perhaps convinced that

Larry would land a job right away and carry away valuable information?) that he granted Larry a year's probation period.

Kranz's method is obviously limited to employees who (1) have really been hiding their light under a bushel and (2) know how to do a selling job in a résumé.

The Tell-Me-Why Approach

Some superiors will not tell a man *why* they are firing him. Instead they will go out of their way to say only very positive things about him. Either they feel so badly about the situation that they can't bear to say anything negative, or they feel that lavishing compliments on him is the quickest way to settle the matter without getting any back talk.

Staying on the payroll under these circumstances is a real challenge. But it can be done.

The president of a medium-sized advertising agency, whose elegance and chic were enough to cow the average man under normal circumstances, had been known to fire several people with the following icy technique.

He would call the employee into his luxurious office that was artfully scattered with unostentatious antiques and costly lithographs. Offering him a cigarette, he would cross the room to light it and say something like, "Well, young man, I see you're making twenty thousand dollars a year. You're really worth more than that. Your talents are too vast for our simple firm. You should be making thirty-five thousand dollars. As a matter of fact, I've drawn up a little list of agencies that I think are more appropriate for you. Want to see them?" he would ask as he waved a tiny handwritten list before the bewildered employee's eyes.

According to the many advertising men he had fired, they had no recourse other than slinking quietly out of the thickly carpeted office, packing up their plants, and going home.

The president might have availed himself of this technique forever had not one copywriter refused to take it laying down.

With the most sincere, innocent expression on his face, the copywriter asked, "Could you please tell me why I am too good for the job I now have?"

Caught off guard, the head of the firm floundered about searching for words of praise. The copywriter prodded him further, nodding and agreeing with all the nice things being said about him.

By the time the interview was over, the young man had talked him into giving him a six-month trial period.

Any subordinate whose superior starts buttering him up for a firing with extravagant praise might try the tell-me-why approach. If it doesn't get the job back, at least it makes an honest man of the boss.

All the employees described who were able to talk their boss out of firing them started looking for new jobs immediately. They say it's essential not to hang around and con oneself into believing that the boss really wants you. Reprieves of this nature almost never last.

They also warn that challenging a superior's decision to fire (with bullying or debating techniques) can boomerang.

The president of a huge Los Angeles real-estate firm agrees: "If a man fights me when I fire him, I don't like it. I'll be polite and listen to him, but my mind is made up. When someone calls up for a reference check, I'll be less likely to give him a good reference. I'll simply tell the truth—which can be damaging to most men fired for cause."

A bad reference is not the only thing one risks in arguing over a firing. The boss who refuses to concede will usually go out of his way to list, clarify, and overemphasize the employee's faults—hardly the best thing for his morale.

Employees confronted by a boss who is not in the least troubled or vulnerable during a firing obviously can't utilize any of the methods mentioned above. Yet they, too, need not remain totally passive. Things can be done or said to make the moment less painful, if not livelier.

You're Fired—I Quit

One way to sidestep hearing a list of all one's faults and misdemeanors is to engage in the "You're fired—I quit" shouting-match so loved by American television. The employee can reap considerable ego-satisfaction from it and possibly avoid the stigma of having been fired. But of course he must be willing to give up all severance and unemployment insurance.

"It helps if the door is slightly ajar and people can actually hear you say you're quitting while the boss blunders about. But if you're buried in a soundproof, carpeted office, the only thing you can do is go to your floor and tell everyone you've quit before the boss gets there. He'll naturally say he fired you if he dislikes you enough. But it's your word against his. I did that. I don't know who believed me. My wife certainly didn't. But the trade press did," said a newly fired investment banker.

Unless a person is certain of finding a job quickly, no one recommends this show of passion—no matter how liberating it may be—for anyone with dependents under twenty-one.

The Nice-Guy Firing

Not all firing interviews are charged with intrigue and shouting. Many are conducted in an honest, straightforward manner.

The superior confronts the unwanted subordinate, tells him exactly why he must be sacked, what the cause is (be it loss of business or some sort of incompetence) and is as helpful as humanly possible. Poised and certain of his position, he is a hard man to try to intimidate.

Many formerly fireds felt that making the boss into a friend instead of an enemy was the only appropriate reaction to this kind of dismissal. So did the bosses.

"When a guy is fired decently—the way it should be done—the only thing he can do is listen to what the boss is saying with an open mind. If he is considerate enough to tell you exactly what went wrong and why, you may learn a lot. Ask questions. After all, he's giving you a free analysis of your career. Why give him a lot of grief? He may be very useful to you someday," said an executive who makes a point of firing people "decently" as well as helping them out later.

Dealing with the Hatchet Man

One nonstraightforward method of firing used by management is to permit a hatchet man (or what advertising executive Jerry Della Femina calls a killer) to do the firing for them.

As a rule, the hatchet man has little real power in the company. He may be the company lawyer or office manager, or he may have a meaningless title in a defunct department. A member of a large conglomerate, who has seen many a hatchet man at work, describes him as "the guy who almost made it, but always got passed over. He hates people and gets a kick out of firing. He especially loves firing people with titles better than his. But he doesn't show it. He's full of sympathy for the guy he's canning and says things like 'You're such an asset to the company I don't know why *They* want to lose you'!"

"He is kept on because he does the dirty work for the rest of the executives. You'll find hatchet men in unstable turnstile operations, high-risk businesses, and of course in companies recently swallowed up by a conglomerate."

There isn't much an employee can do when he is severed by such a creature (as executives who hide behind him know only too well). How can he respond to a suave, impersonal go-between who knows little or nothing about his record? It is of no use trying to bargain for any extra benefits since hatchet men have no real power. And shouting ''I quit'' is a waste of time since a third party—the guy who ordered the firing—knows the truth.

''You can always fall asleep,'' said the man from the conglomerate. ''Look, you know this guy is probably getting a sadistic pleasure out of firing you. If you yell or protest, you're just satisfying his need more. Better to destroy his whole day and snooze while he goes through his plastic little spiel. Rape victims are always advised to go totally inert when they're attacked. It's the same principle.''

Lawrence Bender, an executive recruiter who has had clients come to him bewailing their treatment at the hands of hatchet men, thinks the interview with the hatchet man should be terminated as quickly as possible. ''The guy you're really interested in is your boss, who is using the hatchet man as a shield. It's senseless to waste any time on a patsy like him.''

Leaning forward, Bender jabbed his forefinger in the air. He had seen and talked to more than one executive who had praised God for the existence of hatchet men. He knew management's weaknesses.

''You have to realize that executives who use hatchet men are afraid to confront their employees. And that's what puts the subordinate in a position of relative power.

''Now the worst thing the fired man can do is to go storming in to see his boss in a rage. If he hasn't suddenly taken a trip before he gave the word to fire, he'll barricade his door.

''The best thing to do is write him a note, devoid of anger or passion, requesting to see him. When you do see him, allay his anxieties, don't increase them. He might be so grateful to you for not blowing your stack, he could turn into your best reference. Look, good references and contacts are the name of the game when you're job hunting. Anything is worth trying.''

Another worthwhile ploy is getting the man who is manipulating one's firing, fired instead. This is an intricate maneuver which usually involves equals or near-equals. It is worth mentioning if only because it points up the more diabolical side of corporate behavior. In the following case, the ploy actually backfired.

Getting the Other Guy Fired

Ralph Bingham and Jonathan Schultz were both in their late forties and both contenders for the presidency of a large defense-oriented corporation.

Both ran separate divisional groups within the company. Since Bingham's responsibilities had a larger domestic basis, he had slightly more influence with the board than his rival. But Schultz, known for his enthusiasm and likable, if volatile, temperament, was not without his backers and anti-Bingham friends.

To get the presidency, Bingham knew he had to overcome the Schultz faction. To insure a long and peaceful reign, he also knew he should find some way to dispose of Schultz.

Bingham made his first move by arranging a small meeting with four members of the board and Schultz. Bingham had gathered much data showing how sales in Schultz's international divisions had fallen off. The reason for this downtrend was a dock strike that had paralyzed the whole industry. But these facts were of no consequence to Bingham. For his purposes, Schultz was to blame.

The minute Schultz innocently joined the meeting, Bingham attacked him by saying that poor management was the cause of the low return on investment in his group. Somewhat astonished, Schultz said the matter was beyond his control.

Undaunted, Bingham maintained that other industry groups had not suffered to a corresponding degree. He scattered graphs and charts on the table. Poor inventory control was the real cause. He added that he was only studying the performance of Schultz's group in the best interests of the company—before this small, select management group.

Completely nonplused by the irrationality and gall of his rival's imputations, Schultz began to lose his cool.

He sputtered out sales figures, looked through his own sketchy reports (since he had not come prepared for an attack, he had no real data with him), and rifled through Bingham's stack of incriminating material. Bingham frowned sympathetically and placed a restraining hand on his enemy's shoulder.

Schultz grew more enraged. Pounding his fist on the table and sweating profusely, he (1) lost his temper, (2) used obscenities, (3) accused Bingham of overdrinking and destroying the corporation, and (4) cast aspersions on his colleagues for listening to a bastard like Bingham.

Bingham glanced at his witnesses and fixed Schultz with a chilly stare: "Maybe we should discuss this matter again when you're more in control of yourself, Schultz."

Bingham exited gracefully from the room. The other board members shrugged and followed him out. Schultz sat alone, took several tranquilizers, and shuddered. Without realizing it, he had just fired himself.

Bingham rapidly disseminated the information that "Schultz is acting a little unstable lately, dangerous actually, perhaps he needs a rest," and called upon the other four board members to verify his opinion. In confidence, he embellished upon Schultz' remarks: "He said the reason why the company is in trouble is because there are so many goddamn freeloaders on the board."

After a good night's sleep, Schultz realized that Bingham had actually goaded him into behaving so stupidly in front of four board members and decided that the only way to save his job was to kiss and make up with Bingham.

He stopped into Bingham's office that morning to deliver a reluctant apology. But Bingham was not available.

Later that afternoon, he still wasn't around. It just happened he was on the current president's private plane saying how badly he felt that "a valuable man like Schultz is going downhill."

Schultz was asked to resign in a matter of days.

An older member of the board, who had been pro-Schultz and was wise to Bingham's tactics, said Schultz need not have been fired. In fact, had he played his cards right, he could have gotten Bingham fired instead.

"Schultz's error was accepting Bingham's challenge and playing his game. Once he had made that concession, he wanted to win as badly as Bingham. Without realizing it, he was following the ground rules set up by Bingham when he began slurring Bingham's reputation and trying to defend his group's performance.

"What Schultz should have done was expose Bingham at the outset by *identifying* what Bingham was doing *as a game*. He could have said to the four board members something like 'I hope you realize how foolish Mr. Bingham's accusations are and what kind of game he is playing. Must we sit here and let him indulge in such profitless, time-consuming diversions? Outside factors are the cause of the trouble in my division and there is no reason why I should have to defend myself to Mr. Bingham.'

"And then it would have been good-by Bingham. Once Schultz had straightforwardly shown that Bingham was an undercutting conniver, it would have been relatively easy to convince the rest of the board that they could do without him. No one wants someone around whose play-one-against-the-other tactics are destroying the cohesiveness of the corporation.

"Whenever an employee is dragged into such destructive political activities he should stay cool (especially if there are witnesses around), refuse to play, and then make sure to identify the game for what it is to someone in authority. Once a man is pegged as starting interoffice wars for personal advancement, his days are numbered.''

Confronted by a boss who wants to play *j'accuse*, the employee rarely has anyone to turn to unless he has close and loyal friends well over the boss's head. But when an equal or near-equal such as Bingham is out to get him, he can refuse to play ball and point out to their mutual superiors that time and money are being wasted on company politics. He may just get his competitor fired in the process. Although circumstances for it don't arise every day, this is one maneuver of which everyone should be aware.

Thus far, only cases where firings have occurred in face-to-face encounters have been described. But what about people who never get to see their antagonists? What if he has absconded to Rio or, as in most mass firings, there are too many employees being fired that day for the boss to see them all personally? There is no way a person can get any extra advantages out of an exit interview because there is none.

For these and others, the action—sometimes constructive, sometimes very destructive—starts after the firing, usually in the hours immediately following.

Chapter II

AFTERWARD

When a large drug-manufacturing firm got into trouble with the FDA and two of its major products were bounced off the market, a good 50 percent of its staff had to go. December 15 was departure day for most of them. A fired employee surreptitiously posted a huge hand-lettered greeting on the company's main entrance: "Merry Christmas to every other one of you."

To a person involved in a mass firing, humor frequently seems to be the only recourse. Yet many who have been involved in bankruptcies, shutdowns, and belt-tightening operations, have found other ways to cushion the blows of a collective firing.

Joining Forces

Not too long ago one of this country's largest pictorial magazines went out of business. The publisher took it upon himself to make the announcement personally.

He went from floor to floor in the magazine's building and read aloud a ten-sentence statement describing the financial problems of the business to the assembled employees.

What do you say to the retreating back of a guy who has just taken away your livelihood (and who you *know* is walking away with $10 million worth of assets)? Nothing.

"You get as much cooperation from your colleagues as you can," stated a former editor of the magazine. "After the chairman went back into that elevator, we were all in a state of shock—even though we really knew the closing was coming. Then we all turned to each other and kind of joined together in a united front. Everyone helped out everyone.

We exchanged information about job openings, advised the oldtimers who'd been there sixteen years about job-hunting, and exchanged résumés. The *esprit de corps* was really something. And still is, even though months have gone by since we put out the last issue.''

Being on Exhibit

Another advantage of a mass shutdown is that rival companies know that a lot of talent is loose on the market.

"Later in the day," the ex-editor went on, "the press and television crews came in. It was almost like a party. First we thought they were just there to get information on the folding of the magazine. Then I noticed they were asking people to step over to a corner to talk privately. They were there picking up talent—like vultures. I even heard some negotiating salaries then and there. It was a strange thing to watch, but great for the guys who got picked.

"If I was in a business other than publishing—say in a big bankrupt company like Bon Vivant—I'd get together with the people I worked with and throw a big party. We'd invite all the top executives from other food companies. That way we'd let them get a good look at us—while we got a good look at them.''

Telling the Press

After a shutdown, there are ways to apply pressure on management to render more services than it had intended.

A small family-owned firm went under after a series of disastrous real-estate deals. The owner of the firm, who was still a very rich man, couldn't face the ordeal of announcing the demise of the firm himself.

Safely ensconced in his Connecticut estate and surrounded by bodyguards, he wrote a long, sincere memo saying that

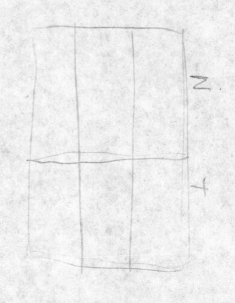

Although Clarence Smith's revolution was on a smaller scale, it was just as much a waste of time and emotion. When Smith was dismissed from a prominent New York brokerage house, three of his colleagues took him down for a drink in the local bar near their office building. Everybody at the t: le felt Clarence's firing had been unfair. They all agreed that their firm was badly run, losing money, and a rotten place to work. Their anger and frustration increased with each round of drinks. At 6:00 P.M.—with Clarence egging them on—they decided to tell the president of the firm what they thought of his cutthroat tactics. By 6:30, they changed their minds and agreed to quit and join Clarence on the street. At 7:00, the president entered the bar with two clients.

The little band of brokers glowered at him, acknowledging his presence with a series of belligerent nods.

The president smiled and waved, apparently oblivious to their hostility. Ten minutes later, Clarence and his group received two bottles of champagne at their table, compliments of the president. End of revolution.

Fortunately most employees recognize the futility of starting a mass walkout, but there are still those who feel compelled to take *some* kind of revenge.

Taking Revenge

"After I was canned, I threw a lighted cigarette down the mail chute of our office building," one young salesman confessed. "I just had to do something. But of course the flame had gone out by the time it arrived at the bottom."

It isn't surprising that so many victims of firing consider revenge. In the old days, if a man stole a cow from you, you'd have to burn his whole ranch down. And an act of adultery merited instant death. Revenge was a question of honor, and the desire for it is still in most people's blood. Which is why practically everyone who is terminated contemplates a vendetta against their erstwhile organization at one time or another. The question is how to go about it.

Occasionally you'll hear about a man who quietly opens a new company next door to the place that fired him and steals all its business away. This is the ideal tit-for-tat. It restores the rejected man's sense of worth and brings a competitive new company into being. It is also carried out months or even years after the day of the firing.

"Revenge is really just the private administration of justice. For it to be successful, it has to be planned carefully and ingeniously so no evil befalls the avenger. If one acts spontaneously, tastes the revenge served up hot, as they say, the act is bound to be petty and hysterical. Or, as in Orestes' case, tragic," commented a professor of Greek literature—which has its share of famous revenge stories.

A placement woman who worked for an employment agency was fired. Convinced that Susan, another woman in the agency, had done her in, she impulsively ordered several magazine subscriptions in the name of Susan Flunky and had them sent to her in care of the agency. Every month *Mademoiselle, Harper's* and other expensive magazines arrived bearing the name Susan Flunky. Susan enjoyed reading them immensely and was indifferent to the change of her surname.

This incident sounds unreal. Yet it happened. People who succumb to revenge immediately after their dismissal don't know what they're doing. And they inevitably end up hurting themselves more than the intended victim.

Other self-defeating revenge actions include scaring the boss's wife with obscene phone calls, writing slanderous graffiti about the company in the elevators, starting a fire alarm in the office building, and smashing the boss's car in the parking lot.

Of course they all get caught. Who else has such an obvious motive?

Every once in a while a revenge story will take a more dramatic turn—but most often in fiction. In the movie *Willard,*

Willard is an office clerk who is wantonly fired by a hard-driving, selfish boss. Willard returns to the office with a suitcase full of trained rats. At his command, the furry creatures leap on the boss's face and body. Bellowing and struggling, the boss backs into a window. As he falls five stories to the ground, the audience cheers. This is hot revenge *par excellence*.

More common in real life is attempted violence, which almost by definition boomerangs. A computer programmer who was fired at four in the afternoon, came back to the office of Thomas Ryder, his boss, with a gun in his hand. It was seven in the evening, the building was practically deserted. "You destroyed my life, now I'm going to destroy yours."

Ryder was able to talk the editor out of homicide and get home safely. He never pressed charges, but neither did he give the man a glowing reference.

If any generalization can be made about revenge, it's a disastrous way to go after a recommendation.

Stealing

Personnel directors and office managers will tell you that the most usual retaliatory act is stealing. Men severed from $75,000-a-year jobs have been known to take a year's supply of white paper, as many felt-tip pens as they can get their hands on, wall hangings, and other miscellaneous objects they think no one will miss.

None of these thefts goes unnoticed, because the office manager is expecting things to be stolen, but he will not bring up the matter unless the losses exceed all limits.

"I don't care about the pencils and paper they take, it's the market reports and files I worry about. While I'm in the process of firing someone, I have my secretary go into his office and lock up his files. After someone reliable has been through them, he can come back and get his personal effects.

I know it sounds brutal. But valuable marketing studies we've paid thousands of dollars for have ended up in the hands of Proctor and Gamble,'' said the executive vice-president of one of America's largest corporations.

Few companies have such paranoid policies. Most don't ask a discharged worker to leave right away, but give him office space and the service of the switchboard some time after he has been severed.

This is a humane and generous gesture on the part of management. It gives the fired person a convenient base from which to conduct the job search and makes the transition from employment to unemployment less traumatic.

It also gives the severed person an opportunity to try to conceal the fact that he was fired. This may or may not be a self-destructive move. Opinion was divided about its feasibility. In rare cases it might work. On the other hand, if it doesn't, the person is exposed as a liar.

Keeping It a Secret

''The day I got fired, I didn't breathe a word about it to anyone. I just went about my business pretending things were normal. In the weeks that followed, I had all my interviews during lunch hour—like any other employed person. Even though I was very bitter over my firing, I kept it to myself. I told myself that I would postpone punching the guys who'd got me fired until *after* I landed a job. I did this for a month and a half and no one ever found out,'' said an executive for a large toiletries corporation who really thinks no one knew.

One difficulty of keeping it a secret is that it requires tremendous control over the emotions.

''Unless a man is very stoical, it's unlikely that he can get through a month and a half of subterfuge without some side effects,'' said Dr. Schmidt, the clinical psychologist.

Keeping It a Secret From One's Spouse

When Fred Longwood was told to vacate his office immediately by the head of an American-run company in Mexico City, it was no secret to his fellow workers that he had been sacked. Nevertheless, the day he was fired, Fred couldn't bring himself to tell his wife. The next day it was even harder to tell her.

For four weeks, Fred got up in the morning at seven, packed his attaché case, and drove off to the center of town—just like a man going to work. In between furtive interviews with other companies, he wandered through the anthropological museum, studying Aztec artifacts and becoming increasingly miserable.

He could get away with his secret because of a shortage of telephone lines in the outskirts of Mexico City where they lived. Since Mrs. Longwood had no telephone at home, she never called him at work. But every evening she asked the inevitable question: "How did things go at the office, darling?"

"And being alone all day with practically no friends in Mexico, she wanted a real answer," Fred moaned. "The strain of making up a whole business day would be enough to make most men collapse."

Eventually his wife heard about his dismissal at the beauty parlor where other company wives had their hair done. This compounded Fred's problem of joblessness with that of "You lied to me—don't you trust me?"

"The best way to tell your wife is to have prepared her for it sometime before. When things look bad for you—or if you can see your company is headed for trouble—let her share your apprehensions. Then if the job does blow up, you can go home that night and simply say, well honey, it happened," counseled a twice-fired civil engineer.

Those who believed that a person should be open about his firing and not try to conceal it, conceded nevertheless that telling people about it was very painful. Probably the worst time to tell people, they say, is the day of the firing itself.

Telling People

An insurance investigator advised that no one tell the news to outside friends while he is still dizzy from the blow of being fired.

"Don't do what I did. After I was sacked, I got back to my office and all I wanted to do was hide. I closed my door and literally contemplated crouching under the desk. You remember the end of that Fellini film 8 1/2 where Mastroianni crawls under the banquet table? Well, that's how I felt.

"Something told me that to counteract this horrible feeling, I should do the opposite of what I wanted to do. So I got on the phone and called every single person I knew and told them what had happened to me. I thought I sounded carefree and full of confidence.

"But I found out later from my friends that I was slightly hysterical. Apparently I was stuttering and incoherent. They said even my voice seemed different—too high and squeaky."

A young lawyer decided to tell his secretary right off. "After I came out of the senior partner's office, I decided the easiest, simplest thing would be to tell her before I started emptying my drawers. She acted like I'd been sentenced to the electric chair—just the kind of response I didn't need that day."

Often, it isn't necessary to tell co-workers the news. They already know. The problem then is how to confront them.

"Everyone knew I'd been canned (my dear supervisor had told them all in advance). But I wanted to find out how they stood on the matter and even approached some of them. But it was useless. They treated me like someone with a horrible disease—like an untouchable. Others—the ones who had been instrumental in having me fired—suddenly felt *guilty*. They couldn't look me in the eye and would kind of slink away

when I came near them,'' said a television writer recently
fired from a national network.

So what do you do? Go into your office and put a quarantine
sign on the door? ''Get out of the office and get smashed—and
don't come back until you and the situation have cooled down,''
the writer counseled.

Getting Smashed

An incredible number of people felt the only way to end
the day of a firing is in a bar. To drink and drink heavily—except for the most determined teetotalers—is expected. A rau-
cous, staggering performance through the taverns and bars
in town has an almost heroic quality to it.

People involved in a mass firing are the jolliest. They have
all those people to drink away the day with.

When it was announced at 10:00 A.M. that a New York
corporation was ceasing all operations, everyone turned to
his co-worker with the same thought: ''Why didn't they wait
until after the bars were open to tell us?''

An employee got on the phone and called a former associate
who had escaped to another company three months before
the shutdown. He told her the situation and in half an hour,
she was wheeling in two urns full of Bloody Marys.

For many, the camaraderie lasted until ten the next morning.

''Look, you drink at a funeral to relieve the tension. Well,
a firing is the same thing—a funeral,'' said a man who slept
in the office that night.

''I suppose there's nothing wrong with getting intoxicated
that day—so long as it's confined to that day,'' conceded
Dr. Schmidt.

But one still wonders, is there anything constructive a person
can do that momentous day? Must he just sit there passively
sedating himself with alcohol?

Challenged by these questions, personnel manager Everett Hardin offered a list of affirmative actions:

What to Do the Day You're Fired

(1) Don't call your old girlfriend or boyfriend. Ex-lovers never understand.

(2) Don't try to write a résumé. You're in no condition to do anything that skillful.

(3) If you decide to write a long letter to someone, don't mail it.

(4) Don't tell yourself that you don't care. You do.

(5) Don't say the word "fired" or any synonym for it. If you do, you'll choke on it. Say you're temporarily unemployed or freelancing. Everyone will understand.

(6) Don't make any long distance calls or send any telegrams at your own expense.

(7) Don't tear up your files.

(8) Don't buy a ticket to Tahiti unless you're sure it is refundable.

(9) Don't contemplate suicide, a heart attack, or a nervous breakdown. The first you can put off till later. The other two will come if they come whether you contemplate them or not.

So much for Mr. Hardin's positive advice.

Only one man, John Rhodes, a professional fund-raiser who has been in and out of several nonprofit organizations (which usually don't pay for unemployment insurance), suggested a concrete, affirmative action that the newly fired might take.

Go to the Bank

"The very afternoon he is sacked, a guy should race to the bank and take out the biggest personal loan he can get. If he's already got a loan, he should re-finance it. He is probably still listed as being on the payroll and the bank doesn't know he's out of a job. But he has to do it right away. Once he's off the payroll, no bank will touch him.

"If he puts the money in a savings bank, he can even earn a little interest. You'd be surprised how stashing away a few thou can soothe troubled nerves. Because money—or rather the lack of it—is what firing is all about."

Not everyone may want to execute Mr. Rhodes' bank loan maneuver (especially those involved in a well-publicized mass firing), but it's a rare person who isn't in full accord with his last sentence. There's no question that after the shock and the hangover have worn off, the first question for the unemployed to face is always money.

Chapter III

MONEY

William James once wrote that "lives based on having are less free than lives based either on doing or being."

This is the kind of high-sounding statement that's bound to titillate the solvent and secure. Promising romance and freedom, it conjures up pictures of itinerant minstrels swinging through medieval castles, Thoreau, and early Jack Kerouac.

Yet when a person is fired and the time comes to base his life on doing (looking for a job) and being (unemployed), the tyranny of having becomes insidiously appealing.

As he shells out savings and cashes in stock, money is the fired individual's first, most practical problem. Before he even thinks about the job search, he has got to be clear in his mind how much money he has, how he'll handle it, and how long it will last.

Ryan's Financial Plan

Meredith Ryan, financial consultant to some of Manhattan's wealthiest widows as well as many middle-income upwardly mobile types, says making a rough draft of a financial plan for the jobless is elementary. Being realistic and sticking to the plan are the difficult parts. This is what she suggests:

(1) Establish minimum salary requirements and estimate how long it will take to find a job based on the experience of others in your field.
(2) Add up all your savings, severance, and potential income from unemployment insurance, freelance, part-time work, spouse, and other sources.
(3) Divide the above total by the number of weeks or months you plan to be job-hunting. That's how much

money you have available to spend per week or per
month.

(4) Make a budget and resolve never to exceed it.

(5) If you don't find a job during the estimated time period,
lower your minimum salary requirement and take the
first job you can get.

Minimum Yearly Salary

Just deciding upon the minimum salary is an important,
emotional decision.

Executive recruiters are always complaining about people's
unrealistic salary demands. "What your ego feels you're worth
or the amount of money you need to keep the kids in prep
school has nothing to do with your actual worth," states management consultant Harvey Christiansen.

"Determining one's proper salary should be no different
than pricing any other product on the market. Supply and
demand are the only factors that should be considered," he
says, emphatically rapping his pipe on his desk.

Many employment agents believed that the unemployed job
hunter should always take a salary cut—except in really boom
times.

Mitch Stenbuck, who dehires as well as recruits executives,
was adamant about it. "Most people—especially those in the
higher brackets—who have been fired for incompetence or
any other cause, should immediately take a pay cut. If they
were up there making fifty G's on merit, they wouldn't have
been expendable.

"What's more, if a man says he wants fifty thousand and
won't take any less, he may have to wait up to six months
to get a job—and make only twenty-five thousand that year.
Whereas if he had come down to thirty-five thousand in the
beginning, he might have been able to work all year and make
a full thirty-five thousand.

"There are other advantages to asking for less," Mr. Sten-buck added. "For instance, an executive making thirty-five thousand isn't expected to produce as much as one earning more and he is less likely to get knocked out on the street when things get rough."

Frank Laser was laid off from his forty-thousand-dollar-a-year job as a marketing executive for a medium-sized New York firm. He was 59. The first thing he did was to sell his hundred-thousand-dollar house in New Jersey.

"I wanted to be in a position where I could afford to work at one-half the salary I had been making. I had to forget about earning forty grand again (I had never been anything but a moderate success in what is a very overcrowded field). I also knew that most companies would make me retire in six or seven years. But until my wife and I were eligible for social security, I had to make some money.

"Whenever I went on interviews, I told them that I had sold my house and was willing to take a pay cut. I didn't want to give the impression that I was a high-living executive or that I was too proud to take a step down. They simply would not have hired me if I had."

He got a job for twenty thousand dollars a year within six weeks.

Deciding on a realistic, possibly lower salary requirement may shorten the time spent looking for a job, but it isn't the only factor involved.

Estimating the Unemployment Period

There is no mean time of unemployment. Everyone's situation differs widely. Almost anywhere in the nation, an executive secretary can find a decent job within a month. Whereas someone fired for having a hand in the till could take from a year to forever to find an equivalent position.

A look around at the unemployed in one's own field should give the average person an idea of how long it takes to get hired. If the person is willing to relocate to areas where there is greater demand for his talents, obviously he'll get a job faster. And the converse is also true. Another important factor to take under consideration is the quality and extent of one's contacts in the business world.

"If a person is a graduate of the Harvard School of Business, he has so many contacts among the business élite he should be able to find a job within a couple of months," says Mr. Christiansen. "Whereas a self-made man from a small unknown firm has to hustle to get his name spread around."

After one weighs every problem and arrives at a reasonable time period, according to Meredith Ryan and many other cautious souls, one should add another month or two to the estimate. "It reduces the temptation to panic and prevents overspending," she said.

Savings and Severance

Horace Volini was given thirty-five hundred dollars in severance and profit-sharing when he was sacked by a California brokerage firm. He cashed it all in and went on a spree in Las Vegas. In two weeks, he went through every penny and returned to Los Angeles broke, hung over and desperate.

"When I had all that money in my hands, I had to spend it. I rationalized that I could make money gambling, but I was like a babe in the woods in Vegas."

Volini's case is an exception. But other fired individuals who have been miserly for years have been known to start dining compulsively at the costliest restaurants, buying expensive clothes, grossly overtipping, and getting rid of their liquid assets as fast as they can.

By making themselves penniless, are they forcing themselves to be obliged to take the first job that comes along? Are they consoling themselves for their firing? Or are they just like kids let loose in a candy shop with more money than they ever had?

"I've never been able to figure out what makes some people more extravagant than others," says Mrs. Ryan. "All I know is that if a person can't handle his money, he should tear up his credit cards and turn his cash over to a friend, a relative, or someone like me who will dole it out week by week. In the case of Horace Volini, I'd have sent him to Gamblers Anonymous the minute he started making noises about going to Las Vegas."

Volini offers this belated advice: "If your severance runs into the thousands, put it into a savings account where it's harder to get at and earns a little interest.

"If you happen to own a lot of longterm growth stocks and don't need extra cash, trade them in for some high-yield stocks and earn something on them. That's what I would have told my customers—if they were fired—to do. Every bit of income counts."

Even income from such embarrassing sources as unemployment insurance counts. No matter how much a person has in liquid assets, almost everyone agrees that accepting some kind of government aid—if one is eligible—is the only sensible thing to do.

Unemployment Insurance

For the prestigious, it is profoundly embarrassing to be seen slipping through the bureau's doors by a member of the country club. The postman's real or imagined smirk as he sticks in the weekly check is another private nightmare.

But income is income and no matter how much cash a person has, his right to receive benefits is undeniable. His former company and his own taxes paid for it, and he should collect.

In most states, the more people a company fires, the higher insurance rates it has to pay. Not to collect deprives one of that small revenge.

The former vice-president of a New York investment firm found standing in line to be the worst part of accepting government aid.

"It was agony for me. There I was, wearing a custom-made suit, with an impoverished street cleaner in front of me and a sixty-year-old librarian with cataracts behind me," he groaned. "So I decided to wear blue jeans and an old ratty ski sweater every time I went down there. But inevitably I had an interview that day. What was I going to do? Change clothes in a phone booth?"

Apparently the only group with no reservations about collecting unemployment insurance are actors. In fact, those who qualify for it are an élite group in New York. In that state, a person has to work at least twenty weeks to collect. In thespian circles, anyone who can get twenty weeks' work in a year is a successful professional.

Many people have mistaken notions about eligibility for unemployment insurance. Some think getting severance disqualifies them. Yet in most states a person qualifies for benefits the very day after he stops working. Whether he gets zero severance or five thousand dollars worth, he should contact his local office the day after he was fired.

One very down-and-out junior executive thought he had to wait thirty days before collecting in New Jersey. He just "heard it somewhere." One ten-cent phone call would have informed him that he could have been getting seventy-five dollars a week. Of course, waiting time may vary from state to state, and compensation differs with individual salaries, but it makes sense to find out where you stand as soon as you can.

Freelance

One way to increase income is to do freelance or consulting work, if one is lucky enough to be in a field that lends itself to that kind of work. Besides creating income, it can be someplace to go in the morning where (unlike interviews) the jobless know they won't be rejected.

An out-of-work editor who freelanced for four months said he greatly enjoyed it because "it made me so aware that I had a concrete skill. I know I can pick up any piece of copy in the world and somehow make it better. Just knowing this gives me more confidence."

Some people have survived so well on consultant work they have never returned to nine-to-five jobs again. Others have quickly made themselves indispensable and become permanent employees.

Although anyone who is lucky enough to get freelance work will usually grab it, many discovered that it was more of a problem than a solution. Since it means being on call at all times, it can mess up the job-hunter's schedule.

For some, freelance can be too difficult. A top-level copywriter was hired two days a week to write little twelve-line ads for a small book publisher. Throughout his career, he had been thinking up major twelve-million-dollar ad campaigns for national advertisers. Those little book ads had him so stymied, he found himself wasting precious, job-searching time trying to master them.

Even though a young architect was grateful for any freelance he could get, he complained that it alienated him from the other workers. "I never saw the finished product. I was paid on an hourly basis for this amount of work and no more. It was very demoralizing."

Menial Work

If freelance is demoralizing, what about menial work for the formerly wined and dined white-collar worker?

"It's not so bad," said the former vice-president of a small glassware factory. "I was out of work for nine months and had nothing but debts. So I became a short-order cook nights. I got a real bang out of having two eggs frying, the toast toasting and getting coffee to the counter without spilling it in four minutes flat. It was good for me. Isn't that what Mao Tse-Tung is pushing? Manual labor for intellectuals? I think it is a great idea."

Many who took menial jobs favored night work such as baby sitting, parking cars, bartending and working as hotel clerks. Night jobs, being less desirable, are easier to get and they reduce the chances of running into business associates while wearing the uniform of one's temporary trade. Night jobs may offer a pay differential over similar day work, and they also leave the daytime hours free for interviewing.

An unemployed stockbroker stuck out a low period of the recession by driving a cab five nights a week. The job solved more than his financial problems. He was able to overcome a growing drinking habit. As he explained it, he knew so many other brokers who had also been laid off that he had started seeing them every night and drowning his problems in camaraderie and extra dry straight-up martinis.

Sara Jean Summer, who at 28 had risen to be a ten-thousand dollar public relations writer in Atlanta, was abruptly let go when her firm lost two clients. She decided that it was time for her to move on to New York City. Her only problem was that her savings totaled two hundred dollars. So she became a maid—but not just any kind.

She mimeographed several flyers announcing the new Sunshine Cleaning Service. For a fixed amount of money, Sunshine Workers would scrub, dust and vacuum your apartment like new. The flyers gave the distinct impression that a cast of thousands was behind this housecleaning project.

Asked how she, who had once sat in a plush corner office, felt about being a maid, she said: "Do you know that most people cleaned up before I got there because they were afraid of what Sunshine Workers would think of them? Usually I spent only an hour in each apartment. In three months, I had enough money to live in New York for six months. Of course, it was more or less tax free,'' she drawled.

Others have found that resurrecting a former trade or skill is the answer. Because it is familiar, a person has more confidence in such work. In fact, doing what one did when younger can make one *feel* younger.

One engineer, who had grown up in the streets of East Boston, reverted to his profitable but shady former trade right in the plant that fired him. His boss, who told the story, said that two hours after the engineer was fired, he was back in his superior's office with two men's suits over his arm. It seemed that they were hot suits given to him by a fence in Cambridge. Would the boss be interested in purchasing one? "Feel the fabric. No labels, but you can tell they're quality. Look at those inseams." He failed to make a customer of his boss, but sold five suits to his peers in the company cafeteria within a week.

A lawyer who was a camp counselor in his teens, organized a Saturday day-camp for the kids in his neighborhood. A school superintendent who was formerly a grade school teacher, tutored underachievers three hours every afternoon.

Filling in the hours between job interviews with any kind of work seems to be obvious and logical. But many unemployed executives will wait until they are down to their last nickel before they'll stoop to menial work.

A young product manager who was unemployed for a solid year said he preferred to borrow from friends rather than take a job outside of his line of work. "I knew there were jobs shoveling snow or selling shoes, but I had this terrible feeling that once I took a job like that, that's where I'd *stay*. Forever."

Spouses and children don't encourage the unemployed to dally in the blue-collar or menial trades either. The executive short-order cook said that his two teenage children were so embarrassed by his temporary occupation that they begged him to find a diner well outside of town.

An unemployed film director from Chicago was offered a job as a chauffeur. He would only have to be on duty five hours a day, but would pick up one hundred dollars a week. No go. His wife made him refuse the job on the grounds that it was degrading and not worth the money. What was the alternative? "I'll work," she declared.

Spouse Effort

To some men who have been supporting their wives all their working lives, the thought of the little woman bravely going out to work is humiliating and threatens their masculinity. Yet many wives feel differently.

"When my husband got fired, I decided to go to work in a travel agency. He didn't feel threatened since my initial salary was minuscule. I had a ball and learned a trade. Long after he found a job, I kept working. Now I have my own agency and make close to what he's making. It doesn't bother him because I broke him into the idea of having a rich wife slowly. Sunday mornings, we drink champagne in bed," said this happily married working wife.

Many people felt that the best thing about having a spouse working is that it gets at least one of them out of the house. "If we had to sit staring at each other all day, we'd have gone berserk," said a woman whose children are in college.

For people with very young children in areas where no day-care center is available, the working-spouse solution is far from easy. "I stayed home and took care of the kids while my wife did secretarial work. I learned a lot about housekeeping and all, but I never want to do it again," confessed a laid-off auto salesman.

Married partners who have always both worked have an easier time of it. One couple—both corporation lawyers —whose combined income is over sixty thousand dollars a year say that the security of two salaries helps them feel stronger and more sure of themselves in their respective jobs. "We never worry about getting fired," she said.

Alice Laughton, a fashion designer who knew she was in a precarious, competitive field, always maintained a profitable greeting-card shop in a suburban shopping center. Though she hired people to work in it, she managed it at night. It was, as she put it, "my security blanket. I always told myself that if I ever got fired, there'd always be the shop."

When she got married, she sold the shop and invested her time, money, and effort in her marriage. "George became my second job. When I got fired three years later, he supported me as well as the shop would have. And I know that if he got laid off, he'd let me support him."

"Don't forget to mention how the kids can help out," a currently employed chemical engineer added proudly. "Until I landed a job, my daughters contributed half of their babysitting money to the family budget. They never felt so adult and important in their lives."

Having explored all possible sources of income from consulting work to a dollar here and there from the kids, the next move in Ryan's plan is to add it all up and divide.

Adding and Dividing

"When you're doing this adding," Mrs. Ryan counsels, "be sure not to cheat. For instance, one client of mine, who has done picture-framing for friends as a money-making hobby, estimated that he could make one hundred and eighty dollars a month doing this in his basement at night. But through the years, the most he'd ever made in one month was sixty dollars. How was he sure he could increase his clientele to the point where he'd make more? I told him not to depend on more than fifty dollars a month. The same cautious attitude should be maintained for estimating cash resources. If a man owes one thousand dollars in pressing unpaid bills, he's got to deduct that first."

Making the Budget

Most people have some kind of budget already worked out. Cutting it and slicing it down to the bare minimum is the subject of another book. One point that concerns us here is that of expenses necessary to the job search.

Job-Hunting Expenses

Donald Rogers, who now works for Westinghouse, told the New York *Times*, "My brother-in-law works for a public relations firm, and when I was having trouble getting a job, he told me to use an IBM typewriter and to use special twenty-pound paper for the résumés. Then I bought a Brooks Brothers suit and had my hair cut, and in two weeks I had three offers."

Whether or not such trust in externals is merited is debatable. But certainly none of the things on which Mr. Rogers spent his savings could have hindered his getting a white-collar job.

He was right about the smart-looking résumé. A grubby, smudged résumé typed on a fifty-year-old Underwood is as self-defeating as ring-around-the-collar.

If a person doesn't feel like typing out each résumé separately, a list of offset printers can be found in the Yellow Pages. Average cost, including typing, should run fifteen dollars per hundred copies.

Not everyone needs a new Brooks Brothers suit, but people looking for work will usually invest a certain amount of money in grooming.

Some older men find that dying gray hair back to a more youthful color is a small but not impractical expense. "Tell them to use one of those products that dyes the hair gradually," pleaded Fifth Avenue barber Sam Molini. "And for God's sake, advise them to leave some gray hair—for verisimilitude. Some guys get so carried away they look like Rudolph Valentino."

Almost everyone needs to spend a little money on a new article of clothing—if only for a brave new tie or scarf. Others need to overhaul their job-searching costumes, top to bottom. "No one wants to hire a beauty queen," remarked personnel manager Everett Hardin. "But a neat outward appearance counts when there's less than an hour to make an impression. It's symbolic of an orderly, efficient mind."

Unless one has use of the former company's switchboard, it is almost imperative for the job-hunter to have an answering service. Secretaries hate to keep calling a phone that doesn't answer. And they will frequently stop calling it and try another number on another résumé. This is particularly true for lower-echelon jobs.

"With a service, there is no need for the children to pick up the phone between nine and five, thus sparing the future employer a monosyllabic conversation with the job-seeker's five-year-old," Mr. Hardin observed.

Of course, the disadvantage of a service is that one risks the dreary possibility of calling up at quarter to five and being cheerfully told by the operator, "No messages at all—all day."

Useless Economies

One of the worst economies is to allow one's physical appearance to deteriorate. A certain comptroller insisted on walking to all job interviews to save on carfare. Since it was summer, he inevitably showed up with a wilted suit, dust-covered shoes, and a wet, shiny face.

Cutting down on cleaning bills and rationalizing that no one will notice that spot in artificial lighting is another poor, pennypinching idea. Others are avoiding the barber or hairdresser, wearing darned socks or snagged pantyhose, and nicking the face rather than changing the razor blade.

Some job-seekers think they are saving money by restricting themselves to eating in greasy diners. Stu Boyd, a media salesman for *Good Housekeeping,* is so violently opposed to what

he calls the "Nedick's Syndrome" that if any of his friends
are out of work, he gives them a three-week membership
to the Yale Club in New York. There they can get good,
inexpensive meals at the grill and make contacts with men
who are working. "Just because these guys are out of work,
they feel like leeches on society with no right to eat decently.
But it's a false economy. How can they make contacts unless
they're seen in the right places?" argues Mr. Boyd.

Not many job-hunters are lucky enough to have a friend
like Boyd, but the point he makes is applicable to everyone.
Showing up occasionally at the clubs or hangouts of the
employed and influential is the smartest thing a job-seeker
can do. Maybe he'll have to drink draft beer and fill up on
pretzels instead of lunch, but he is being seen and staying
in circulation. As Stu Boyd says, "Sticking one's head in
a cup of inky black coffee at a formica counter isn't going
to get a man anything but the smell of grease in his clothes."

Excessive Spending

High-level executives are very vulnerable in this area. Only
they call it "keeping up appearances." Giving up the trappings
of power such as a chauffeur-driven car and three private
phones is an uncomfortable experience.

One deposed executive vice-president hired a temporary typist with an English accent to come to his home and place
his job-soliciting phone calls for him. When the girl got his
party on the line, he would keep the person waiting for two
minutes before he picked up the phone.

Others can't face the fact that there is no more expense
account. They make a big fuss over saving receipts whenever
they go out (which is often) for a costly meal. Since entertaining
for job-hunting purposes is not a legitimate tax deduction,
the gesture can only be nostalgic.

Lowering the Minimum Salary

If the end of the estimated unemployment period has come and a new job has not, Mrs. Ryan's advice is to lower the minimum salary and "take the first job you can get."

Some disagree and will borrow from friends or family. Still others decide to retrain for an entirely new career. Whatever decision one makes, it's not especially helpful to contemplate it in the days immediately following the firing.

"Even countenancing such a possibility is a discouraging and negative way to think. If a client comes in moaning about how he'll never find a job, I tell him to shut up. Like that. I yell it. I want him to feel ashamed of his lack of confidence," said management consultant Harvey Christiansen.

Ashamed or not, thinking positively is the only way to be thinking at this point in the fired man's odyssey, because after the budget has been faced and completed and the newly fired is more or less at rest about what he can spend, the next bit of paperwork on his desk is the writing of the résumé. And for that endeavor, a positive, self-aggrandizing, ambitious, self-loving—if not self-worshiping—state of mind is imperative.

Chapter IV

THE RÉSUMÉ

Jason Littlewood, a thin young man with a receding hairline and horn-rimmed glasses, was a magazine editor. He was bright enough, accomplished enough, and just stylish enough in his English-cut suit and Gucci loafers, to be any publisher's dream. When he was laid off from one of the major news-magazines, he was positive he would find a job at once.

He whipped together a résumé listing all his major editorial jobs and assignments and took it with him everywhere he went.

During one particularly grueling interview with a forty-years-a-veteran-in-the-newspaper-business, he began to have serious doubts about himself and his curriculum vitae. After staring at the latter for fifteen minutes, his interrogator puffed on his cigar and growled, "Tell me son, what is the best piece of work you have ever done in your whole life?"

Jason named one article he had put together, then remembered he hated its conclusion and took it back. He mentioned another, but added that he had grave doubts about its political bias. Finally he told his interviewer that he'd have to think about it. Could he send an article to him?

"Of course, I never sent it," Jason said later. "The interview had gone badly from the start, but my hesitation over what was supposed to be my favorite article really clinched it."

After three weeks of thinking it over, he still didn't know what article he was most proud of. But he decided not to worry about it. "I'm a damn good editor and can pull any article through from start to finish better than most men. And on my résumé, an employer can see how incredibly broad my experience is," he said bravely.

But is being "damn good" and "broad" sufficient for the serious job-hunter? Does a random listing of his achievements and experiences on his profile give him anything resembling a competitive edge on the job market?

Mitch Stenbuck, who has been in the recruiting business for as long as anyone in Boston can remember, says No. When he heard about Littlewood's plight, he leaned back in his Barcelona chair and pontificated on the subject of résumés and image-making for an hour. "Everyone out there claims he is damn good at some general thing. But what an employer wants to know is what can Littlewood *really* do? Can he get a heartbreaking article out of some nutty kid reporter who is willing to go on the front lines in Vietnam? Does he have a way with press agents? Why was Littlewood being paid? How is he different? That's what they want to know. If this Littlewood's résumé had shown any unique qualities he might never have been asked that question about his best article to begin with."

To clarify his point, Stenbuck described one of his recent clients: "Name of Ted Clements, father of two, Ivy League type. He was brand manager for five years with a big detergent company. He'd introduced a couple of interesting products in test markets and had one that went national.

"His only problem was that he got a little cocky and started going over his boss's head. Eventually he got the sack for it. He's intelligent, well-spoken, efficient—and a dime a dozen. His résumé read like he'd been stamped out of a machine.

"I tried to get more information from him about his career, but it didn't work. He kept telling me he knew how to 'run a tight ship.' Finally I told him to go home and think about himself and write a résumé that had some character in it. It's the best way to find out who you really are. He rewrote it. We discussed it. Finally he had an outstanding résumé. But I'll tell you more about Ted later.

"People think a résumé is just a collection of facts. I say it's a creative act. Because selling yourself is really an advertising problem that demands a creative solution."

The Résumé as an Advertising Problem

For the successful solution to their personal advertising problems, Stenbuck refers all his clients to *Reality in Advertising*[1]
by Rosser Reeves, formerly the chairman of the board of Ted
Bates & Company, a New York-based advertising agency.
In this book Reeves discusses how to tackle the advertising
of all mass-produced products. He admits that many products
seem identical, but contends that real differences exist either
in the product itself or in its use. It's just a question of searching
hard and digging deep enough to find it. This may involve
trips to the factory where the product is made, long consulta-
tions with the people who invented the product, and poring
over the trade journals, but eventually it is possible to find
what he calls a unique selling proposition.
According to Mr. Stenbuck, this is the crux of all advertising
problems: saying something unique and persuasive. "If every
guy looking for a job thought of himself as a loaf of bread
in search of a slogan, he'd triple his chances of getting hired."
Reeves describes how to go about creating an advertisement
that has a Unique Selling Proposition in three parts.
(1) *Each advertisement must make a proposition to the consumer. Not just words, not just product puffery, not just show-
window advertising. Each advertisement must say to each
reader: "Buy this product and you will get this specific
benefit."*[2]
Ads that do not make such a proposition to the consumer
are the kind that say: "Tasty, tangy, tempting." "You'll be
glad you asked for ———. It's so incredibly smooth." "More
people use ——— than any other."
A man searching for a job often describes himself in similarly

---

[1]New York: Alfred A. Knopf, 1961.
[2]Ibid., p. 47.

nonspecific, stereotypical terms. Littlewood's "damn good" and Clements's "run a tight ship" were product puffery.

These descriptions mean nothing to the buying public or the hiring superior.

(2) *The proposition must be one that the competition either cannot or does not offer. It must be unique: either a uniqueness of the brand or a claim not otherwise made in that particular field of advertising.*[3]

Reeves explains his point by citing several advertising campaigns, one of which was a Clairol Hair Coloring campaign. Clairol had many consumer benefits: It was easy to use, dyed the hair safely, and was so natural-looking that people weren't able to tell whether the hair was tinted or not.

Ted Clements also had several talents. He was an expert on marketing analysis, a veteran of the detergent business, and knew how to introduce new products. In fact, the detergent he introduced went national slightly more quickly than most new detergents. This fact was partly due to luck and partly to his own nature. Ted liked efficiency and moved quickly.

Jason Littlewood was not without his product benefits either. He was adept at putting together numerous types of articles concerning politics, fashion, interior decorating, and medicine. He was also easy to work with and thorough.

But simply to have a benefit is not enough. A product must have a benefit people really want, says Reeves. There are thousands of unique propositions that do not sell as in the case of the toothpaste campaign: "IT COMES OUT LIKE A RIBBON AND LIES FLAT ON YOUR BRUSH." This was a proposition . . . [that] did not move the public, because it was apparently of no importance to them."[4] Which leads us to the third part of the USP's definition.

(3) *The proposition must be so strong that it can move the millions, i.e. pull over new customers to your product.*[5]

[3]Loc. cit.

[4]Ibid., p. 48.

[5]Loc. cit.

After examining all its benefits, Clairol's advertising agency decided that the one the public most wanted was a dye so natural-looking that friends would not be able to tell whether or not the hair was dyed. Thus Clairol came out with the famous slogan: "DOES SHE . . . OR DOESN'T SHE?"

Since there are many marketing analysts around and even more veterans in the detergent business, Clements decided that his USP should be: "I'm the guy who gets new product introductions through fast." It suited both his personality and his job history and would "pull" management over to hiring him.

Since Littlewood was capable of doing just about every kind of article imaginable, but nothing spectacularly, his choice of USP would be more difficult to come by.

When this is the situation, according to Stenbuck, there is nothing to do but *create* a preference or proclivity that the marketplace really needs. This may require considerable research.

Suppose Littlewood were to discover that there was a real shortage of male home-magazine editors. He would then do well to settle upon the USP: "An editor's editor who can put together home-decorating articles from the male point of view." He would dredge up all his home-oriented articles and present them as his main contribution to journalism. Even if no single one of them was especially outstanding, narrowing down his enormous versatility to one specialty would make him (1) something slightly more unique, (2) easier to understand, and (3) more commercial.

He might also, Stenbuck suggested, beef up his story by citing prizes he has won, mentioning his contacts in the interior-decorating and furniture-retailing worlds, and doing a few freelance jobs in that specific area.

Stenbuck says the best way for a job-seeker to find his USP is first to do "research" on himself: go through old files, review his entire career, examine his personality and contacts.

With all this information in front of him, he should then write his résumé in as many different ways as he can think of. Out of this activity—which may take up to three days (not a long time when one thinks that most ad campaigns take months to create)—he should be able to produce a plausible USP.

After determining his USP, he should write his profile once again.

When Ted Clements figured out who he was and what he was selling, his résumé wrote itself—and it made sense. It had focus. It gave a cohesive picture of a unique individual who fulfilled a need. Instead of describing ten different people, it described one.

"Every job description should portray the man rather than the job and should always relate to the USP. This may demand some tricky, time-consuming writing, but it is possible to make even the worst job seem exciting and pertinent if it relates to the total image he wants to create."

Obviously no one can write on his résumé that he is "the guy who gets new product introductions through fast." But he can get his colleagues and friends to refer to him as "the guy who" if he sets his mind to it. He can also see to it that any letters of recommendation written on his behalf include his chosen attribute, even in different words.

Above all, he should let his employment agents know how he would like to be described. When telephoning prospects or sending out an applicant's résumé, it simplifies the agent's job to have a key phrase with which to describe his client. "When a client and I have finally arrived at his USP, I usually scribble it across his résumé in red pencil. So whenever I send it out, it jumps off the page," Stenbuck confided.

He couldn't say enough about the need for a USP. In the long run, he said, it is actually more important than the résumé itself, "because you know and I know that many executives simply don't bother to read résumés. They look at the height, college, and last name, and ask their secretaries to 'file it somewhere.' The only way to reach those guys is to have a powerful USP that I, or someone else, can communicate quickly on the phone or in a letter.''

Read or unread, however, the résumé still has to be written. One aspect of résumé-writing that stymies some job applicants is the format.

Format

Many pamphlets and books on the résumé format have been written. *Guide to Preparing a Résumé*, put out by the New York State Employment Service, is as good as any. It gives nine sample résumés. Reading them and seeing how others sell themselves (even if the job histories are fictitious) can be very helpful. Reading competing job-seekers' résumés is even more useful if such valuable documents happen to come one's way.

Formerly there was only one way to present the facts. This was to account for every single year of one's life since leaving school. The idea was to camouflage any extended periods of unemployment (or stints in a drying-out farm) by stretching dates of employment or covering them up with mythical free-lance activity. This busy-beaver approach, with its strict attention to chronological order, tends to clutter the résumé with data on irrelevant, unimpressive jobs from the past.

The new look in profiles is to restrict oneself to giving a detailed account of jobs and accomplishments that occurred in the past five to eight years. Jobs held during these recent years might merit a good, solid, eight-line paragraph that lists achievements such as cost-cutting, reorganizing a department, or, as in Ted Clements's case, speed in introducing his new product. Experience prior to the recent past (which may cover anywhere from one to twenty years) is lumped together in two or three lines at the bottom of the résumé, possibly using abbreviated names for former employers and three-word descriptions of jobs.

For some, this may be a great way to cover up an unsavory past. But more important, it shows that the job-seeker's head is where the world is: the present.

No one except the most suspicious bureaucrat is really going to imagine that a man did time in Sing Sing in 1961 if he was a functioning vice-president at IBM from 1964 to 1972. The man's current history is most employers' concern.

Within the résumé format, the job-hunter is also expected to give additional information about health, marital status, and that ever-present *bête noire*, age.

Unless a person is very famous or very beautiful, omitting one's age is a mistake. If it is missing on the résumé, it immediately invites the suspicion that the applicant is either too old or too young for the job. If one isn't happy with one's age, there is nothing to do but write down the age one would like to be and hope to be believed.   People who opt for lying about their age, face different problems. One twenty-eight-year-old advertising man, making thirty-five thousand dollars a year, was way over his head and knew it. When he was fired, he decided that the only way he could stay at his high salary level was to pretend he was in his mid-thirties. To give credence to this fact, he ate his way up to two hundred pounds on the assumption that anyone overweight always looks at least five years older. When he finally reached thirty-five, he was thirty pounds overweight and no one in the world believed that he was a day under forty.

In most cases it is easier to fake being younger than older. Wearing a toupee, taking the Clairol route, submitting to weekly Vitamin B injections, and exercising regularly are only a few of the ways older men succeed in achieving a more youthful allure.

Salesman Leif Atwater (who is forty-five and looks it in spite of all his efforts at rejuvenation) says everyone should check with someone reliable before taking the big step to lie: "If you say you're forty and you walk in looking like you're six years away from retirement, your interviewer's disappointment can kill your prospects from the start. Don't go around asking friends how old you look and never ask a lover. Would you tell *them* the truth? If you've really got the guts to face reality, ask your family doctor how old you look. Doctors are always ready to tell you the worst."

Another standard element of the résumé is the job objective, which is typed at the top of the page near the applicant's name, address, and phone number. This is simply a statement of the type of job a person wants to get and should in no way be confused with his USP. If the résumé is going to be duplicated and sent out to hundreds of people, many feel the vaguer the job objective, the better.

Some job-seekers still put their requested minimum salary on their résumé. Mr. Stenbuck finds this limiting and unwise. "It's like wearing a price tag on your lapel and deprives you of all your bargaining power—mine too, if you're my client."

Style

Employers prefer résumés that sound like they've been written by the man they are interviewing. Yet many businessmen resort to using professional résumé-writers to paint their verbal portraits. These writers rarely convey the personal, individualistic tone the successful résumé needs. What's more, an experienced personnel man can usually recognize an "assembly line" résumé and will find it difficult to respect anyone who can't write a decent one-page report about himself.

"The best way to achieve a nice, easy style is to resolve, before you sit down, to load the résumé with solid facts. Think of yourself as being on trial and told by the lawyer to give only the facts and nothing but. Then the main challenge is finding facts that are interesting and exciting," says Joseph

Germain, personnel manager of a large consumer food products company.

In other words, if Ted Clements's detergent went national in a year, it is interesting to know that his sales in test markets which were $6 million, led to a volume of $20 million on a national scale a year later. Precise figures are something the reader can grab hold of. Hearing that Clements made "stupendous achievements in the detergent field" is not.

"All facts don't have to be totally explicit, though," Germain went on to say. "I enjoy receiving a résumé that excites my curiosity. Take this sentence." He picked up a résumé lying on his desk. "1970–71: Supervised new products division. Experimented extensively with new food additives.'

"I know when I show this résumé to the boys upstairs, they'll be anxious as hell to see this guy and find out just what additives he's talking about. It's too tantalizing to pass up."

One way *not* to tickle the reader's curiosity is to dress up the résumé with phrases like "participated in" or "assisted with." It invariably sounds like the applicant was standing with his hands in his pockets while others worked around him.

Some people have been known to list the year and model of their car or felt compelled to mention their summer jobs during their high-school years. "My mother lives with me. She is sixty years old and can travel. Father, aged seventy, passed away October 10, 1955," was the unhappy last sentence on a résumé reported in an AP article on the job search.

Length

Most business manuals, employment agents, how-to books on job-searching, and magazine articles, all tell the job-seeker to keep his résumé down to one page. This is the cardinal rule of all résumé-writing and wouldn't even bear mentioning if it weren't for the fact that people still don't listen.

There are still sophisticated businessmen around who think three-page résumés are "necessary to give the full story" or "to show that I have a lot of experience." They don't. They look desperate—as though the applicant knows he's no good, but if he crams in enough data, no one will notice. They also look boring, unreadable, and confused. If the president of the firm to which one is applying can have his life crammed into a short paragraph in *Who's Who*—who is the job applicant to presume to fill up three pages with less noteworthy autobiographical data?

People unable to control the prolific urge might consider writing a simple one-page résumé and attaching two or three additional pages of more detailed information about each job. This way, the need to expound about oneself is satisfied, and the employer is not obliged to wade through the material unless he really wants to.

Mailing Résumés

Few people enjoy mailing a résumé cold. It's much nicer to be *asked* "tell us more about yourself." Some employees, like media salesman Stu Boyd, refuse point-blank to send out an unsolicited résumé. "Why send a sales presentation before you've got the package on review? You don't do that in marketing."

Be that as it may, most people, sooner or later, inevitably come up against a help-wanted ad that suggests—or a busy personnel man who demands—the sending of a résumé before an interview is granted.

If one does mail a résumé and is then invited for an interview, it is always wise to have another copy of the résumé in one's pocket to give the interviewer, says personnel manager Peter England. "By the time he arrives at the employer's office, the first résumé might be in the secretary's files—or wastebasket.''

Accompanying the mailed résumé, there must always be a cover letter. This can be the easiest or most difficult thing to write.

The Cover Letter

There are two philosophies about cover letters. One is that it should be no more than six lines long and say practically nothing but I'm looking for a job, here is my résumé, and I'll call you later. This is the least complicated approach, and aside from changing the name of the firm one is addressing, it need never be altered from one mailout to the next. Depending on the strength of one's résumé and reputation, this simplified letter may be the most appropriate for most job searchers.

There is, however, an entirely different school of thought that maintains that the cover letter is twice as effective as the résumé and can say everything better and more skillfully because it is not restricted by the latter's short, impersonal paragraph system.

A strong cover letter is especially useful:

(1)   When the résumé contains such unattractive information as poor health, an age problem, or an erratic career pattern. The idea here is that a snappy letter will make the prospective employer gloss over these details in the résumé and remember only the ambitious and exciting tone of the letter.

(2)   When the person sending out the résumé has been involved in a rather scandalous firing. For instance, when Harry Nichols (described in Chapter VII) was fired for knocking a colleague unconscious, news of

his violence traveled so quickly that an ingratiating cover letter was almost essential.

(3) When the person's accomplishments are so stupendous (at least in his view) that no résumé can do them justice.
(4) When the job-seeker is a good, imaginative letter-writer.

To write a stimulating but coherent cover-letter, personnel manager Peter England says one must:

(1) State rank and duties in one's last, most recent job.
(2) Tell what one can do differently from others (a nicely worded suggestion of a USP might go here).
(3) Imply that one's presence in the company would be profitable for that company.
(4) Name the date when one will call for an appointment.

These statements need not be made in the above order. Unless a person's job title or duties are exceptional, it may be better to open the letter with points (2) and (3). Someone like Clements might start his letter with point (2):

"At the ———— Company, I supervised the introduction of XYZ detergent. In less than two years, sales increased from zero to $20 million."

On the other hand, point (3) might be a better send-off:

"In the last three years, I have been intimately involved with the marketing of a new detergent product. I think it would be advantageous to both of us to discuss the profitable procedures and innovations which I helped to implement there."

No matter where one starts, it is imperative never to be reticent, says Mr. England: "If you did something worthwhile, say so. No one wants to hire a shrinking violet."

Unfortunately many men who have been fired—especially those fired for cause—become very diffident and find it almost impossible to come out with a straightforward, self-aggrandizing sentence about themselves. Positive that everyone is looking down on them, they find it unthinkable to blow their own horn when all their instincts are telling them to lay low.

To remedy this problem, England suggests, "They might consider writing the first draft in the third person. Writing about him or her creates a certain distance and lessens people's urge to be humble." Whatever the writer says, it is vital to capture the reader's attention from the start: "No matter what he writes, he should never start his letter with the words: Enclosed is a résumé of . . ."

Using the Résumé

Besides mailing them and carrying them from one interview to the next, it behooves the job-hunter always to have a few crisp tidy résumés somewhere near the top of his attaché case at all times. Everywhere—on the commuter train, over lunch, standing on the steps of the Public Library—he should be ready to put his beautifully written curriculum vitae in the pocket of any individual who might know of a job lead.

"One of the most effective ways to make a person remember you is to give him a big piece of paper with your name on it," says public relations expert Hank Snyder.

Which brings us to the next most important item on the fired man's priority list: the cultivation of job contacts. Once the résumé is written and the sales story has been put together, most of the job-hunter's time will be spent searching for middlemen in the job market among friends, associates, and superiors.

"Knowing how to use contacts—to manipulate them, if you will—is essential to the job search and can make the difference between one month or six months on the street,"

Snyder declared. Most formerly-fireds heartily agreed with him and were more than cooperative in giving tips on the handling and creating of job contacts.

Chapter V

CONTACTS

Bernita Jones, a promising executive in a music publishing firm, was riding in a cab with Jim, her immediate boss, and the president of the company.

In the course of their discussion, the president used the expression, "Well I don't give a shit!" Realizing that Bernita was sitting next to him, he apologized for his language.

She smiled sweetly and said, "That's all right, I don't give a fuck!"

Both men winced.

That afternoon, Jim called her in and fired her. She begged for a reason. He explained that although he didn't agree personally, the president said he wouldn't tolerate a young woman in his corporation who used language such as Bernita had used.

Bernita thanked him for telling her the reason and fled. Forty-eight hours later, the absurd story of her firing was being chuckled over by almost everyone in the music-publishing world. Bernita was not one to keep things to herself. In no time she amassed a small army of loyal friends for whom getting her rehired was something of a *cause célèbre*.

Armed with a good repeatable story of injustice like Bernita's (as with people involved in a well-publicized mass firing), intermediaries for the job search appear in droves.

But for most severed individuals (whose story can be capsulized in one dreary word: "incompetent," "negligent," "laid-off"), the search for good job contacts is a difficult and time-consuming process.

So as not to expend too much energy on this search, the first question they must ask themselves is: Who is a good contact and who is not?

Some believe that every human being has a potential job

lead inside him that's dying to get out, and the only way to tap it is indiscriminately to cultivate everyone they know. A designer recently fired from a job in the fashion industry, said, "The day after I was fired, I went through my address book in alphabetical order and called everyone in it. And every single lead anyone gave me, I followed up within a week."

Depending on the length and quality of one's address file, the designer's democratic approach may be feasible, but by far the majority of job-seekers prefer a more selective method. Rather than haphazardly courting every friend and acquaintance since childhood, they feel there exists a certain hierarchy of job contacts.

The Hierarchy

Based on most formerly fired employees' observations, the best job contacts, in their order of importance, are:

(1) A client
(2) Men one or two echelons above the job-seeker
(3) Employment agents
(4) One's peers
(5) Newspapers and the trade press

The worst are: friends, neighbors, and relatives.

Once the job-seeker's priorities are established, he must now begin to nurture and develop his contacts—not to mention flatter, cajole, pat on the back, and occasionally feed them.

For having a few decent go-betweens is only a small part of the struggle for the fired job-hunter. The most crucial part is *activating* the contacts: getting them to the telephone, the typewriter, or the informal lunch that will lead to a significant job-interview or offer.

"Every contact must not be approached in the same way," says Roger Greenburg, a twice-laidoff sales representative who revels in the whole subject of the "contact game." "If you meet the president of ITT at a golf tournament, you don't entertain him with a long story about the raw deal you got on your former job. Whereas mentioning it to an old buddy who knows a *vice*-president at ITT might be very appropriate."

A little probing among currently and formerly fired people proved that Mr. Greenburg was not the only one who frankly relished this Machiavellian side to the job-hunt. "Getting people to go out on the limb for you is the ultimate test of diplomacy," mused a corporation lawyer.

How then does a person make people become his emissaries in the job hunt? As Mr. Greenburg says, everybody must be handled differently.

A Client

"When I got fired from a certain women's magazine, I turned to my best friend, who also happened to be the president of one of New York's largest ad agencies," said media salesman Sam Horan. Ad agencies buy space in magazines. Sam's occupation was to sell space. Motivating his friend to help him was easy: Their children were soon to be married. Sam's only problem was to let the world of journalism know that he had a live agency president in his vest pocket.

"I convinced my friend that we should be seen in public places together. Since he loves a good, long lunch, we decided to make the 21 Club our base of operations. The day of our first appearance, we ran into the publisher of a very, very well-known magazine at the bar. We invited him to have lunch with us. Over the steak tartare, we chatted about ad revenues and other subjects related to the business very amiably. Not a word about my being out of a job was mentioned. When the coffee came, I got up and left them alone. That way my friend had twenty minutes to tell the publisher what a fine man I was. He called me the next day, and of course, I got the job.''

Unfortunately most people's jobs are so removed from their industry's clients that it is impossible for them to meet them. But for those in communications, law, and other service fields, where client contact is frequent, the client is the *ne plus ultra* of all job contacts. It takes a lot of doing to mess up the situation. Horan recommends, however, based on his own successful experience, that the job-seeker:

(1) Always put the client contact in touch with someone high up in the corporate hierarchy.
(2) Give the client some time alone with the top man. It shows you trust him.

Since few people who have a close and binding relationship with a client get bounced, the case of a fired man having a client as a contact is exceedingly rare.

The majority of jobless people consider themselves lucky if they know men in the second preferred group of contacts, what Greenburg calls the "cream of the crop."

People One or Two Echelons Above

These demand more attention, agility, and time from the job-seeker than anyone else, for it is from their ranks that the man who will eventually hire him comes.

Of this group, many found that their last boss was the best source of leads.

The Ex-Boss

As we observed in Chapter I, most superiors feel intensely guilty about firing someone—so guilty that, if the organization can afford it, they will pay agents to dehire their employees. If they lack funds for dehiring, many still feel they should do their utmost to relocate any subordinates they let go.

"Every time I fire someone, I feel a moral obligation to try and help him to get a job—and that includes real incompetents. You know, incompetents have families too," said an executive in the shipping business who was better known for his hardboiled business attitudes.

But not all superiors feel so guilty that they are driven to phone their friends and associates and ask them to consider hiring their severed employees. A second exit interview may be required.

The second exit interview entails writing or calling up the former superior and politely asking him if he will have lunch or a drink, or see the job-hunter in his office to discuss his career. This may occur anywhere from three days to three months after the firing.

Roger Greenburg was especially helpful on the subject of the second exit interview.

"Your request to see him should be made calmly, with no rancor and just enough self-confidence to show you haven't gone to the dogs *already*. Nine times out of ten, he'll see you. Just knowing you're alive and cool and finally making some sense, will make him generous and expansive. He might even pay for the lunch, but don't let him. Go dutch. You don't want to be a financial burden on him, you want to be a *moral* burden.

"The meeting should start with you asking what he thinks of your career, prospects, what you did wrong, etc. Now that he has you out of his hair, he might give you a truly honest rundown on your abilities—which may or may not be helpful to you. But it doesn't matter. The important thing is for him to clear his conscience by getting everything off his chest and for you to appear to respect his opinions. With you sitting there being so friendly and together, it's almost impossible for him not to finally ask, 'Where have you been interviewing?'

"At this point you might mention some particularly abominable company and ask him if he thinks it would be a good place to work. Caught in the paternal role (in which you've placed him), he won't be able to keep his mouth shut. Inevitably he will tell you that you are making a big mistake and that he has friends in four or five far superior corporations. If he doesn't offer to recommend you to these friends, ask him to. If he still hesitates, ask him if you can use his name."

If Mr. Greenburg's ploy does not work, another way to activate the former boss is to play on his vanity. "Ask him how a successful man like him would approach the job market at this time. Whom would *he* contact if he were you? What would *he* say?" suggested an executive in the automobile industry.

"If he is the competitive type, tell him about all the other contacts you have in his class. He might just want to outdo them in kindness—and show that he has more influence than they," suggests a corporation lawyer.

"Whatever you do, don't play on his guilt. Don't tell him that your kid has been mugged because you can't afford to send him to prep school any more. He doesn't want his guilt increased, he wants it relieved. Helping you get a job will relieve it. Hearing that your life is going to pieces will increase it and make him run the other way. A man can stand only so much remorse," said a division manager who was plagued by mournful phone calls from a father of six whom he had fired.

One rule of the second exit interview is never to argue with the boss. "Sure I see guys for lunch after I fired them. Why not? I want to find out how they're doing. But many times they tell me they want my advice—and then they spend the whole lunch telling me why I was wrong to fire them. Obviously I'm not going to help any man who sits there telling me what a schmuck I am,'' said the salesmanager of a major lumber company, who claims to have helped place many of his more docile ex-employees.

''The best thing about getting a lead or recommendation from one's former boss is that it removes most of the onus of being fired. It almost seems that you've been let go because *he* did something wrong, not *you*,'' concluded Mr. Greenburg.

Going back to a former employer for help is not always advantageous. Sometimes the ex-boss hates the man he sacked so much that he is delighted the latter can't find a job. Or in the case of a bankruptcy or shutdown, he may be too busy looking for employment himself to assist anyone beneath him; in that case his recommendation isn't worth much anyhow.

When this is the situation, the job-hunter must look elsewhere to establish contact with his preferred management level.

Freelance Contacts

If he has successfully done freelance work for anyone, the next most obvious person to go to is the man who ordered the freelance. Like the ex-boss, his recommendation carries weight since he has had firsthand experience with the job-seeker's work.

Freelance clients often tend to be less critical, since they had less time to observe the job-seeker. But they also are fairly passive in their help since their involvement is minimal.

''I was almost wiped out after six months of being out of a job,'' said architect H. G. Paulson. After freelancing with one of California's top architects, however, he finally got the latter to recommend him for an exciting city-planning project in Latin America. He tells contact-seekers to ''have long talks with your temporary boss; ask his advice. If you can't get to him at the office, invite him home to dinner. Since there isn't such a rigid chain of command in the freelance situation, it's easier to make the boss a friend.''

Clubs

Alumni groups, clubs, and professional associations are excellent sources for finding upper-level contacts. Many of these have placement bureaus. Registering with them should be automatic.

"Go to all their cocktail parties, meetings, and lectures, and circulate," says a Yale graduate and member of two professional clubs. "If they ask how you're doing, get right to the point. Never meander at cocktail parties. Things move too fast. Motivate them by recalling mutual friends, interests, and former ties. If they ask you to call them, try to memorize their phone numbers without writing them down. A ready pencil in a small room puts people off. And naturally, stay soberer than anyone else in the room."

Service People

Bankers, lawyers, stockbrokers, and other people in the service businesses may have several clients, one or two steps ahead in the pecking order, whom the job-hunter wants to see. Coaxing introductions out of them is fairly easy. Their motive for wanting to get their client back on his feet is obvious.

Making them use their judgment is trickier. "Check out a lead carefully from anyone who works for you in a service capacity. They may just be leading you down a primrose path in an effort to please you," said a marketing man who went on four fruitless interviews arranged by his thoughtless but well-meaning lawyer.

Interviewers

People one meets during interviews can often produce job leads. A retail buyer advises the job-hunter, "Use your interviews for getting names. If you know Macy's isn't going to work out, ask the guy who's interviewing you how things are across the street at Gimbel's. If he knows anyone over there, get his name. Ask what he's like. Try to get him so interested he'll place a call to the Gimbel's guy.''

Sometimes the person doing the interviewing will suggest other leads of his own accord—just to get out of a touchy situation. ''I had a very unsuccessful interview with a research manager of a large consumer-products corporation. Most of the time he was on the telephone and he barely read my résumé,'' recounted a young female package-designer. At the end of the interview, he wrote down a list of four executives in four other companies and promised to call them all. He did. I saw them and snagged two offers. I found out later that his company had a strong bias against hiring women. Rather than be picketed or face a lawsuit, he did his best to get me hired by someone else fast.''

''Be careful you don't get bounced around like a pingpong ball. Sometimes one of these personnel managers who can't bear to say no will pass the buck to his lunch partner who works in another company. If you feel that's his game, ask him *why* he thinks you should see his friend Sammy down the block,'' cautions Roger Greenburg.

Former Employees

A member of the Forty Plus Club (an excellent association to join for anyone in that age group) advises older men who have come down a few rungs through the years to call up any former employee who has shot ahead of them. ''If you were a decent boss, they'll be pleased and proud to help you out. And they'll remember you better than anyone else.''

Thanking Them

After following up any of these job leads, it is not a bad idea to write a brief letter thanking the intermediary, says one promotion manager, Larry Schultz. "Unless my contact was a buddy I saw every day, I always sent thank-you notes— nothing fancy—it was usually handwritten on my personal memo paper. Even if the guy sent me on a real bummer, I thanked him. When I was out of work, I figured the more my name crossed anyone's desk, the better."

Agents

The next category of preferred middlemen are personnel agents. Although some may only be making twenty-five thousand dollars to the job-hunter's former sixty thousand dollars, they are on intimate and confidential terms with executives making twice as much as both of them. Lacking friends in the upper echelons, job-seekers will find these the best people to know and cultivate.

Agents, however, present a very special problem for the job-seeker. Their social behavior may be unusual. Take, for instance, one of New York's top executive recruiters, who happens to be very thrifty. One of his economies is to take résumés sent by people who are of no use to him, tear them into four equal parts, clip them together, and use the blank side for memo sheets. When he has to give a job-seeker a name or address, he will write it down on one of these makeshift memos. "My god, I turned over the sheet of paper he gave me and saw part of someone's life on the back!" exclaimed one shocked applicant.

This story is atypical, but it exemplifies one of the most conspicuous traits of the personnel agent: his tendency to treat clients as commodities rather than people. Whether they are recruiters, management consultants working on retainer, or smalltime employment agents with picture calendars on the walls, they all stand to make money on people they place in a job. That doesn't mean that they can't be kind, understanding, crafty, and helpful. It just means that the trading and selling of people (flesh-peddling) is their business, and knowledge of that reality influences some of their actions.

Another trait they share is remarkable indiscretion. They would prefer to think that they themselves never gossip and that they only listen to the dirt others bring them. But often, to elicit a juicy story, it is necessary to give a little something in return. As a matter of fact, outside of the old Hollywood columnists, they are probably the worst gossips in the world—at least the best of them are.

Nevertheless, in recent years their prestige and usefulness has increased considerably, and they are valuable catalysts in the job market. Anyone who eschews them is probably missing out on many good leads.

Activating agents requires some skill, especially when it is a buyer's market. Although a job-seeker may register with as many as twelve of them, it won't do him any good if his card is buried in the files. Job-seekers who have successfully motivated agents came up with these suggestions on how to make them consider their causes over everyone else's.

(1) Don't lie to an agent. If you were fired, say so. Let the agent decide if it's possible to fake it without being exposed. The same goes for shading the truth about past professional experience.

(2) Don't call and pester them every day. They'll call you fast enough if they have some good news for you.

(3) Keep all appointments you agree to go to.

(4) Don't accept double referrals. If Agent A sends you to IBM, don't let Agent B do the same. Forgetting who referred you where creates bad will, complicates fee arrangements, and gets you a bad name with all agents.

(5) Go out to lunch with your best agent and listen to his life story (usually rags to riches). They like to talk about themselves. This may be frustrating when you're

anxious to talk about your own problems, but they've heard stories like yours so often . . .

(6) Look and act organized. They are universally impressed by the applicant who gives the impression that "finding a job is a job in itself." Read up on the background of corporations which you apply to and tell the agent what you learned. Remember names. Allude to your "correspondence file."

(7) Listen to their advice even if you don't intend to follow it. These guys are sometimes a little power-mad and don't like to be contradicted.

There were conflicting points of view on how much a person should and could confide in an agent. "Be honest with them. Don't be afraid to tell them when you're down or hesitant. They enjoy being amateur psychiatrists," says executive recruiter Lawrence Bender.

Others disagreed. "Talking to an agent is no different than interviewing for a job. It's essential not to appear fearful or lacking in self-confidence," said an executive from the auto industry. He cynically added, "Of course if you're in a very high salary bracket, you're more likely to get their sympathy. If they straighten you out, think of the fee!"

An agent who works mainly with investment banking firms in lower Manhattan says, "Sometimes I'll try to build up a guy who is down and seems to have lost his confidence. It's kind of like giving him a moral transfusion. But you know something? He usually collapses six months later even if he gets a job."

This may not be true of all men who seek moral support from agents but it does seem to point up the fact that encouragement from a less commercial, more professional source may be more effective.

On the selection of an agent, Mr. Greenburg advises, "Don't listen to negative things anyone says about a particular agent. If he's in business, someone likes him. Go and decide for yourself whether there is any chemistry between you. Even if your peers all hate him, he may be the right guy for you.''

Which points up one of the main problems about colleagues and peers as contacts: So many of them simply don't know what is good for their fired friends.

Peers in Business

To begin with, they don't know as much about the job market as the average man on the street.

"In two weeks of actively shopping around, I knew more about the state of the publishing business than any guy who was holding a job. Not only did I pore over the trade press looking for leads, I had recently been inside ten or more firms and found out what was going on,'' said a formerly fired senior editor in textbook publishing.

The area in which a peer is most knowledgeable is his own company. "If he is in a large company with several openings on his level, he might be willing to divulge considerable information on how to approach his firm. If, however, he feels that I am after his job, he'll either clam up or feed me a lot of misinformation,'' continued the editor.

As a rule, peers become less and less helpful the higher up the corporate ladder one goes. There are never enough jobs to go around at the top of the pyramid and the relationship between equals becomes more competitive, if not unpleasant. "Would you befriend Jim Aubrey if you were a television-network president?'' asked a vice-president in the communications industry.

If a colleague has left a former job voluntarily, he might be more than willing to introduce the job-hunter to his old boss. Under these circumstances, the fired peer is no threat.

Another way to make use of peers is the double-referral method. This is a complicated maneuver discovered by Roger

Greenburg which, he says, almost never fails to get a man a profitable interview. "Say you know a certain Mr. Bradley who is two levels above you. You met him at a dinner party or he's an alumnus of your university. The most obvious thing to do is call him up cold or write to him asking to see him. The more intelligent thing to do would be to search around among your friends and peers for someone else who knows Bradley. You then get him to call Mr. Bradley and tell him that you are a very valuable item. If this person is too busy to call, ask him if, when you call Bradley, you can say he suggested it. It's a curious psychological fact, but hearing that a second party (you being the first party) is interested in your welfare will enhance you in Bradley's eyes."

How does an out-of-work man motivate peers to render these small services?

"Put a little fear of God in him. Tell him you'll do the same for him when the day comes when he'll need your help," suggested an out-of-work lawyer.

"Don't in any way appear to be competing with him. Respect the sovereignty of his position," cautions personnel manager Everett Hardin.

"I never waste much time with people I consider my equals when I'm looking for a job. One half hour with them depresses the hell out of me. If they can't give me a decent lead after two five-minute phone calls, I forget them," said a jobless and disenchanted film director.

Newspapers and the Trade Press

Most job-hunters find answering help-wanted ads alienating and demoralizing. "What can you say to someone when you don't know who they are?"

Fred Lichfield, a direct-mail specialist, advises the job-hunter to think of an ad as a test market for one's résumé and standard cover-letter.

"If they 'pull' (get a quick response), you know your letter and résumé are all right. If they take weeks to answer or don't answer at all, you know you're sending out a loser."

Some job-hunters prefer newspapers to any other type of intermediary. "They're great for out-of-town jobs, if that's what you want. And getting a job through them means you did it all on your own, without having to pull any strings. Besides, when you answer a blind ad you have no preconceived notions about the company you're writing to, so there's less chance of being disappointed."

As for writing a situation-wanted ad for oneself, two rules seem to apply to everyone.

(1) The job-hunter should have someone else write the ad. "No one knows how to advertise himself except Muhammed Ali. And often even he makes a mess of it," says Larry Townsend, who, though he is a copy-writer, would never write his own ad.

(2) It's a waste of money to buy an ad when the market is already glutted with people possessing the same skills and background as the advertiser.

How can a person activate a newspaper? "You can't, unless your sister happens to be in the advertising department and can accidentally put your ad in bold type. Or tell you who is placing the blind ads," said a man who threw away two hundred dollars on ads for himself in the Los Angeles *Times*.

One group no one seems to have any trouble activating is that which most people consider the worst possible job contacts.

Friends, Neighbors, and Relatives

Many job-hunters say that this group should never be used for procuring introductions. But if the job search lasts long enough, they eventually succumb.

A friend, without meaning to, can be very condescending in his help. If a poker-club member calls up an executive friend and says, "My old pal just got fired, would you see him a few minutes?" this can be the kiss of death.

A serious interview should never start on the premise that it will be terminated in "a few minutes." If it is, you'll inevitably end up exchanging useless remarks about your mutual friend and nothing else.

Employers don't like social references, either. "If a guy calls me and says his golf partner is looking for a job, I simply won't see him. I'd rather have the golfer come to me on an impersonal basis. Then no one is obligated to anyone and I'm not conducting business like some kind of dating agency'," said marketing director Tom Kramer.

Probably the worst are relatives who want to help. "Either way you lose. If you go to see the guy your relative—in my case, my father-in-law—suggests, it's bound to be a waste of time. Don't ask me why, it just always is. But if you don't go to see them, you're in worse trouble. Then they say you're not trying or you are just too high-hat to accept their help," said the son-in-law of a small-town banker. He interviewed every prominent citizen in Moline, Illinois, before he landed a job in Chicago—from a newspaper ad.

"Occasionally a relative will be of real help. But I've never heard of one who didn't gloat about it for years—the 'I got that boy started' type of thing," said a forty-five-year-old executive who actually did get his first chance in investment banking through his uncle. But to everyone who knows his uncle, he's still "that boy."

Paul, a young man whose father is one of New York's foremost lawyers, got his first job in engineering on his own steam. When he was laid off, he decided to accept his father's help. Although he had a respectable two years of experience under his belt, he was in no way prepared to deal with his father's friends, most of them heads of corporations and miles ahead of the young engineer. All but one interviewed Paul, out of respect for his father's reputation. But because each was a very busy man, these interviews were preceded by hours of waiting time. And often his appointments were canceled at the last minute. In every case, he was referred to lower-echelon people (one of whom eventually hired him). But he calculates that he spent at least eighty hours of wasted time seeing his father's buddies.

But does Paul really know? Perhaps years from now one of those company presidents will remember him and he'll take ten leaps forward.

As in all the advice compiled here, there are infinite exceptions. Sam Horan's best friend was a client. Someone's aunt may be Joan Crawford. An ex-boss will smile and advise and give a man a damning, slanderous character-reference. There will always be dead-ends and amazing breakthroughs. It's up to the job-hunter to intuit which are which.

To assist this intuitive process, job-seekers were asked to name those qualities to look for in the ideal job contact. They came up with these random descriptions.

The Ideal Job Contact

(1)   Someone who is not flirting with your wife or husband.
(2)   Someone who's not a blabbermouth who will recommend you but then casually mention that you were fired because of your violent temper.

(3) Someone who thinks you're too modest to do a real selling job on yourself.

(4) Someone you're not ashamed of. For instance, a bookie may be the chairman of the board's best friend, but do you really want his recommendation?

(5) A person whom you owe money. In fact, anyone who stands to make money if you get re-employed.

(6) A man who is respected for his judgment in the business world.

(7) A person you don't mind feeling grateful to.

Having delineated the ideal job contact, who is the ideal job-seeker these people want to help? For this, Mr. Greenburg has the last word: "Nobody, I mean nobody, is going to help someone who looks or acts like a loser. It's embarrassing to recommend him. Whenever you're with potential contacts, look well-groomed, talk sense, and keep your breath clean. Look and act as you would on an interview."

But how does one look and act on an interview?

Chapter VI

INTERVIEWING

"I only knew Gerlach vaguely through the Princeton Club, but I wanted him to make me part of the palace guard he was forming over at the D—— Corporation," said executive treasurer George Connell, describing how he got the biggest job of his career. "Someone told me he went to the barber over at the Waldorf-Astoria, so I bribed the head barber to tell me when Gerlach's next appointment was and asked him to give me a seat next to him. With that bib around his neck, he was a captive audience. Since he had nothing better to do, he was willing to listen to me drop names and say good things about myself. By the time the barber was shaving his neck, he had asked me to have lunch with him."

If only all interviews could take place on such neutral grounds. Unfortunately, most interviews are conducted on the employer's territory with *his* secretary feeding him phone calls, *his* application forms to fill out, *his* well-thought-out questions to answer, and *his* window throwing harsh light on the applicant's eyes. And the latter feels more like a salesman with his foot in the door than a responsible future employee.

Yet people do occasionally enjoy their interviews and manage to manipulate them to their own advantage. One way to get the upper hand is to be prepared for almost every contingency through rehearsing.

Rehearsing

Few people ever rehearse for anything except before the bathroom mirror. This is better than no rehearsal, but not as good as doing it before a live person.

Interviewing for an undesirable job is one method of rehearsing. During such interviews, the applicant is bound to be more relaxed, more apt to listen to himself and study his own techniques and responses. The only catch to this is that a person may do so well that he will end up being offered the job. Then he's up against the decision to accept immediate income or hold out for a job of his liking.

By far the best rehearsal is in front of a close friend who knows something about the job-seeker's line of work, and is willing to be honestly critical and tell him *everything*: whether he crosses his legs too often, if he is prey to conversational tics like saying "you know" five times in one sentence, and how genuine his answers sound.

The person who profits most from rehearsals is one who has lost his self-confidence and whose nerves are showing badly. James Quest, a vice-president with American Home Products and a firm believer in rehearsals, tells this story of his friend Marshall: "Marshall was sacked from a big job with one of the tobacco companies. Friends had told me that he was in bad shape, but I didn't realize how bad until I met him one morning on the New Haven."

Marshall told Jim he had an interview at nine-thirty that morning. As he described the job for which he was interviewing, he kept nervously toying with the *Times*. In ten minutes he had the front page in shreds. When the conductor asked for his ticket, he jumped halfway out of his seat. He was the living, breathing example of what the free-enterprise system can do to the emotionally insecure. More than that, he was scary. No one could look at him without thinking, "This could happen to me."

Jim told Marshall to pull himself together. But Marshall barely heard him: He was too busy tearing up page 3.

"Marshall, I don't think you should go on that interview today. Cancel it."

"Cancel it? How can I? If I don't get that job, that's *it*. I'm finished. Do you know that I can't even pay the taxes on my house? That my wife made French toast for dinner last night and before that we had baked beans? I've *got* to get that job!'' he hissed.

Not until they had arrived at Grand Central Station had Jim convinced Marshall that the job interview could wait and that something must be done to help the latter overcome his near-hysteria. Jim didn't hope to instill waves of self-confidence in Marshall overnight, but he did have a modest hope that by rehearsing, Marshall could at least manage not to *show* his panic.

Marshall postponed his interview until the following Monday and agreed to get together with Jim and run through a few mock interviews over the weekend. That Saturday, out of the hearing of his wife and children, Marshall sat with Jim on wooden crates in a deserted barn on his property and went through the most grueling session conceivable. When Marshall hesitated, Jim would bellow, "GET TO THE POINT.'' If he apologized for any shortcomings, Jim would stamp his foot on the straw-covered floor and say, "Don't tell me what you can't do, tell me what you *can* do.'' In between these attacks, Jim pointed out ways in which Marshall could camouflage his low self-esteem.

Monday morning, shaking inside but not outside, Marshall went to his meeting. Compared to Jim's treatment of him, his interviewer was a pussycat. He didn't get that job, but he did get the next one that came up.

Few people are as shattered by unemployment as Marshall. But that doesn't mean that rehearsals are not valuable to everyone. Being well prepared and in control of one's responses, brings one closer to what personnel agent Mitzi Morris calls "the seventy-five-thousand-dollar-and-over bunch''—in her mind the ideal interviewees.

The Ideal Interviewees

"It's a pleasure to send them out on interviews," she says, "because I always know that the employer will call me later and tell me what a good impression they made—even if they aren't right for the job. The reason why they interview so well is that they have been up in the front lines longer than most people. They know how to fake it. They can control their emotions. They have learned how to take a great deal of pressure, otherwise they would never have gotten into such a high salary bracket. And in the interviewing situation, they are cool, no matter how down they feel. They're professional about themselves and objective about their work."

Even if a man is rehearsing for a seven-thousand-five-hundred-dollar-a-year job, it isn't a bad idea to imagine himself as one of Miss Morris's executives and to try to convey the same buttoned-up impression. One of the ways to achieve it is to be able to handle the most trying aspect of the interview—personal questions about oneself—intelligently and unblushingly. Some questions most frequently asked are:

(1) What went wrong on your last job? (Why were you sacked?)
(2) What are you most proud of in your career?
(3) What do you consider your main weakness?
(4) Where do you want to be five years from now?
(5) What did you like best about your last job?
(6) Do you get along with people?

It's a rare interviewer who covers all these questions, but having a ready answer for them can't be disadvantageous.

What Went Wrong on the Last Job?

If the applicant was laid off, the answer is obvious. But when a person is fired for cause, it gets stickier. (Lying and saying he quit when he didn't is almost impossible to get away with if one has any dependents or if the unemployment period occurs during a recession.) Some people will be blatantly honest about it: "I got fired because my reports were always late." Others won't, because they sincerely believe that the future employer does not want to hear the naked truth: "I was pushed out to make room for the boss's nephew." Everyone will concoct his own story with varying degrees of plausibility and ingenuity.

"If you're fired from a place with a lousy reputation, like most telephone companies, you should imply that you were the victim of a plot," says the vice-president of a car-rental firm. "Project the idea that you were threatening mediocre management. Depict yourself as a hero, but be very specific about your accomplishments and the causes you had to fight for. Insinuate that their backward attitudes were the real cause of your being fired.

"If you're fired from an organization like ours, that's known to be a growing, vital place, it's tougher to explain away. First capitalize on the fact that they actually hired you. After that sinks in, you can admit that you fell down on the job. Then right away, reassure them that you have done something positive to restructure your life and make you employable again.

"Tell them that since your divorce, your attitude towards work has changed. Or that after having taken several night-courses you are better equipped to handle problems. To some more liberal employers, you can even admit that you've been through psychotherapy. If you're candid enough, they might end up consoling you for being fired."

Many job applicants may find these suggestions dubious and defensive. An alternative approach to the what-went-wrong question was offered by James Jordan of Batten, Barton, Durstine & Osborne. "State why you and your boss didn't see eye-to-eye in simple, objective terms. Then, admit that your view might be biased and suggest that I call your boss and check his side of the story. You'll sound reasonable and mature and fair.

"One thing that really turns me off is when a fired employee paints a totally black picture of his last boss. No superior can be that much of a bastard. When a guy talks that way, he immediately brands himself as being unreasonable and difficult to work with."

A great number of fired personnel depend on the tried-and-true "personality conflict" explanation. Just because it is so familiar may be the best reason for not using it.

What Are You Most Proud of in Your Career?

The answer to this question was covered in Chapter IV. If a person has worked out his USP while writing his résumé, he should have no trouble giving a concise, articulate reply.

What Do You Consider to Be Your Main Weakness?

"Answer this queston by mentioning a weakness that may possibly be construed as a strength," says Jim Quest.

Typical answers: "I get so many ideas, I sometimes go off the deep end and my boss has to pull me back in." Or, "I'm hard on my subordinates because I make them work as hard as I do."

Where Do You Want to Be Five Years from Now?

"In the Bahamas on my own forty-foot yawl. Where do you want to be?" a young college graduate replied. She got the job. She was also young and pretty.

The standard "In five years I want to be where you are," might do for almost anyone—but what if the man doing the hiring is a little paranoid?

Probably the safest answer and blandest is, "Well ahead of where I am now."

The worst answer is, "Running my own business."

"That's like asking me to hire a viper who will take away all my clients," said one executive who got just this response from an otherwise perfect interviewee.

What Did You Like Best about your Last Job?

Getting boringly factual at this point can break the momentum of the interview. So can being too enthusiastic about the last job, if only because it invites the question, "If you liked it so much why aren't you still there?"

The easiest way to handle the question is to revert back to the USP and mention one duty that relates to it.

Do You Get Along with People?

The answer is obviously Yes. It is a wonder why anyone bothers to ask this question, yet they do—perhaps just to judge the reaction of the job-seeker. If this is the case, a sad little smile regretting the good times back at the old shop is not out of keeping. Perhaps an anecdote about a lifetime friendship with a former boss could be added to that Yes. Or mention could be made of an intensely loyal employee.

The list of possible questions is endless and finding the right answer for all of them is impossible.

When a stockbroker was asked how long he had been married, he replied, "Seventeen years." He had no idea his interviewer would come back with, "Isn't that a bit too long?"

The president of the brokerage house interviewing him believed that his employees' lifestyle should be comparable to his firm's dynamic love-'em-and-leave-'em approach to business. John, a loyal husband, flunked when he replied, "But I love her." But by then he didn't want the job anyhow.

The Job-Seeker's Questions

It is often said that the first half of the interview belongs to the employer. The second half gives the applicant a chance to ask his own questions.

If he has boned up on the company he is interviewing, he has a real chance to shine at this point. Employers are very impressed by questions that highlight the company problems (and give the job-seeker an opportunity to mention how he solved similar problems in a former job). The more familiar he is with what is going on in the company, the more he appears not to need extensive training. This already makes hiring him seem to be a saving.

Having a friend within the company is helpful when trying to cook up good, meaty questions. However, much data can be had through reading annual reports, proxy statements, Standard & Poor's, and Dun & Bradstreet reports.

The applicant might finish with a few inquiries about advancement within the company, benefits, stock options, and—if it hasn't already been brought up—salary.

Fully prepared with questions and answers and a dream of himself as part of the "seventy-five-thousand-dollars-and-over bunch," the fired man is ready to stop rehearsing and start interviewing.

The Interview Itself

Many formerly-fireds and men who hire offered several random suggestions on how to act and react during these very important confrontations.

"Never answer a question with a question."

"Don't sit through the interview with your coat on. It looks like you expect to be escorted out in five minutes."

"Avoid garlic and mouthwashes. One offends, the other plants suspicion of a drinking problem."

"Give yourself plenty of time to get there. One thing I hate is for a guy to rush in like he was just completing the fifty-yard dash. Christ, you can hear him panting during half the interview."

Almost all agreed that one of the hardest things to handle during interviewing is one's emotional attitude.

"Try to love your interviewer," says a California industrial relations man. "After a guy's been out on the street for a while, he usually walks in prepared to hate the man that's interviewing him. He decides that he is going to reject the interviewer before the latter rejects him. He's preparing for a hurt since he realizes that most of the time, he isn't going to get the job anyhow. So he comes in and right off, he notices the tobacco stains on the guy's teeth and sneers at the Herman Wouk books on his shelf. Instead, the job-seeker should be thinking, 'Maybe I could love you if you won me over.' He should ask intelligent, polite questions that draw his interviewer out. When the interviewer tells him some idea he has, he should compliment him and say things like 'I never thought of it from that perspective.'"

"Don't be enthusiastic," warns a top advertising executive. "Enthusiasts are always on the junior level. From people earning a good salary, we want *judgment*. Be a little remote—like your getting hired was something of a joke. Like you don't really *need* the job."

"Interviewing is something like having a first date with a person. It's basically a mating dance," says James Quest. "Both the employer and the job candidate try to make things look rosier than they are. No one exactly lies, but no one tells the whole truth either. The employer tries to make the job seem more promising and the applicant will gloss over his shortcomings and jazz up his achievements. Both try to psych each other out. But the one who plays it the coolest always wins."

A television scriptwriter who was fired during a big network housecleaning operation said he always had a ball going on interviews: "I loved it because I was projecting myself. It was good for my ego, because for an hour or so, I was doing nothing but saying good things about myself. I enjoyed it." Obviously he is a salesman who believes in his product.

If a man comes out of an interview feeling like he has just been run over by a tractor, chances are he doesn't believe a word of his sales story. In that case, interviewing becomes as depressing as trying to sell a barrel of rusty nails. Perhaps the best thing for him to do is construct a new story.

Another cause of post-interview depression has nothing to do with the job applicant himself—it's the employer who is at fault—by being unduly rude or by offering false encouragement.

Rudeness

Far from being a mating dance, an interview can turn into a monumental putdown.

One of the more usual forms of rudeness is talking on the phone while the job-seeker sits in attendance. It puts the latter in a demeaning position and presents him with the immediate problem of what to do with his wasted time. Staring into space and patting the sweat off his brow is the quickest way to make one's carefully rehearsed confidence ebb away to nothing.

"If a guy is gabbing on the phone a long time or conferring with his employees while I'm in his office, I try to assume that it really is very urgent business and try to keep busy with something else. Usually I write in my notebook. I write anything: the color of the guy's eyes, the name of the receptionist. If there's a company manual on his desk, I read it. Short of that, I might walk around the room and look at his paintings. The important thing is to keep occupied and not sit there like a passive lump," says a currently unemployed investment banker.

Other discourteous, morale-wrecking gestures on the part of the interviewer are keeping the job-seeker waiting an hour, gratuitous criticism of his career, relentless staring, long silences, sneering, eating and chewing while the interviewee watches, and asking insulting questions like, "If I hire you, when do you plan to get pregnant?" Or, "Do you really think a man your age can handle what is strictly a younger man's job?"

Employers who have already made up their minds to hire someone else are most guilty of these offenses. But so are men interviewing a person for *their* job (either because they are moving up or out), busy men who would rather not be delegated for the task of interviewing, simple office sadists, and people who feel they have been bamboozled into the interview by outside pressures (a family friend or thoughtless boss). Every time a person goes on an interview, he risks running into one of these types.

"There's not much you can do about it when they start knocking you around," says a jobless engineer, "except get out as fast as you can. The longer you put up with it, the worse you'll feel later. I once ran into a guy who asked me how a man with my puny—that was his word, puny—experience hoped to get a decent job. The question was so unjustified and frankly hostile, I felt I had to do something to get back at him. So I put my feet up on his desk, flicked ashes on his rug, and answered by criticizing the lousy way he was running his business. He was dumfounded. It was very gratifying," said a salesman who, with his Italian suit and evenly tanned face, seemed more than qualified to execute the counter-putdown.

"If you can maintain a sense of humor about your interviews, you've got it made. When I'd come home from my rounds, I'd do imitations for my wife of the people I saw. It put the whole job-searching business in another perspective," said a formerly fired art director.

"Don't brood over a bad interview. Shake it. People who treat a job candidate badly are the exception, not the rule, thank God," he continued.

Rudeness is transient. The job-seeker knows the situation is hopeless, and in a few hours its ugliness can be classified as a bad memory. Far more treacherous are interviewers that lead him on with promises they have no intention of fulfilling.

False Encouragement

A California toy-designer says that his worst experience while job-hunting was with an executive who appeared so impressed with his blueprints, he wanted to hire him on the spot; "I just had to meet a few members of the board in New York and the job would be mine. I had my bags packed and my plane reservations made. When I called to inquire about the exact time of the meeting in New York, nobody would speak to me but a certain Miss Wazewski. My executive was mysteriously unavailable for a whole week. Fifty dollars worth of phone calls later, my wife convinced me to give up."

"The only way to protect yourself against these guys who lead you on is to assume that everyone's guilty until proven trustworthy," said Everett Hardin, personnel director of a large insurance firm. "There are a lot of men in my company who will promise the world to applicants and then ignore them.

Of course, I, as personnel director, bear the brunt of it, since the switchboard operator transfers their calls to me. I tell them as politely as possible to stop hoping—and stop calling. I really feel like telling them not to be so goddamn gullible.''

Nonetheless, cases of rudeness and false encouragement are infrequent, not the rule. Knowing that they are real, if unlikely, possibilities, makes a person less vulnerable. Dwelling on them can drive him up the wall. Most employers are sincerely interested in hiring people they interview—so interested that they ask likely candidates to fill out application forms and take standardized tests.

An executive is rarely asked to fill out an application form until he has clinched the job. On the lower levels, the applicant may be required to fill it out before his interview. No matter when it's done, filling in those blanks should be done with care.

Job Application Forms and Tests

"Forms can be a trap," says Margaret Slamin, personnel director of a large medical center. "You can tell more about a person from forms than from a résumé. With forms, we're making him tell us what *we* want to know—not what *he* wants us to know. If he writes small and puts his whole life history in a small space when you're asking for a quick, one-word answer, he has no confidence in himself. A lot of erasures usually means he's lying to you. So does taking an hour to complete the form."

That's part of the problem: completing it. All of it. Most personnel agents have a bit of the bureaucrat in them, and the sight of an empty space provokes them. As they see it, no piece of information is too humble for their files.

Job-hunters often complain about the three personal and three professional references that are requested on forms. Even if they've been calling their friends every day for ten years, they inevitably forget their phone numbers the minute they're asked to write it down.

In addition to unnecessary probing about one's height, weight, and color of eyes, unfriendly questions like "Have you ever been a member of the Communist party?" have been known to appear on forms. "The only thing to do in this case is take a deep breath, try to believe that the guy who's interviewing you is fighting to get that question removed, and write a strong, indignant No," says executive recruiter Mitch Stenbuck. And, he might have added, especially don't erase here.

Several forms benignly ask the applicant if he has any history of mental illness, for how long, and where he was incarcerated. The answer to this is of course negative.

After each job he lists, the job-seeker is usually asked his "reason for leaving." "*Never* put fired," Mr. Stenbuck begs. "Put 'to seek new opportunity' or something equally positive. Remember those forms go into their files after they hire you."

"People get the feeling that the form is like a legal document and that they are under oath to tell the truth and nothing but. But sometimes I'd prefer that they didn't. I don't really want to know if a guy has had a dishonorable discharge from the army if everything else about him looks O.K. Usually the only thing we check are his last two or three jobs—never his army record. And unless he's a recent grad, we never verify the school he attended," confessed the personnel director of a detergent-manufacturing company.

Various companies ask job-seekers to take aptitude or personality tests before the decision to hire them is made. Some high-minded individuals flatly refuse on the grounds that the company is invading their privacy. The best commentary on these corporate probing techniques is in William H. Whyte's *The Organization Man*. Besides wholeheartedly condemning them, he tells the reader how to pass them.

Taking the tests has two advantages: It makes the applicant appear sincerely interested in the job, and it shows that he is easy to get along with (and therefore easier to work with). And if he knows how to beat the tests, what difference does it make if he takes them?

"If he runs up against a test he's unfamiliar with, he should ask to see the results," advises Mitch Stenbuck. "It may get him back into the company for another interview and can give him an idea of how his talents are being appraised by the computers—something every job-seeker should know. A man out of work should continually be getting information on himself—not just by taking tests, but by writing his résumé and listening to himself when he interviews. Probably the single most positive aspect of being axed is that a man has a chance to get a new perspective on himself."

Most formerly-fireds concurred with Mr. Stenbuck's view. But, many added, the self-knowledge that comes from the mechanical aspects of job-hunting is not the only positive benefit a man derives from getting fired.

During those long hours between interviews, there's much a person can learn about himself, much he can do that he never did before, and many new people to meet. There's a whole other world out there to experience. And most of it is surprisingly positive.

Chapter VII

THE POSITIVE SIDE

Sam Baruch was head of new-product development in a small midwestern chemical company. He'd been with the firm for twenty years and had gone to the same winter resort in Florida for an equal number of years. He had had the same friends since college and had been carrying on a tepid affair with his secretary since he was thirty-three. Then his company unexpectedly merged with a conglomerate, and Sam lost his job. When asked how his firing had affected him, he blushed and became apologetic. "It was nothing that would mean much to anyone else. They were small, unimportant things." He didn't want to discuss them, but two bourbon-and-sodas later, he grew more expansive.

"First off, I learned that my wife was glad I was out of a job, so she could have an excuse to go back to work, and that my youngest son hated me. Let's see, what else? An old friend of mine and I got drunk one night and he informed me that I dressed like a hick. I also discovered that I could get by another year with my Ford and that my wife had known all along that I had been having an affair."

Finding out what's really happening around them is not the only thing people are reported to have learned when they are fired. Some pretty startling insights about one's work habits and basic career goals have been known to emerge. Things they could never have faced while working suddenly seem confrontable.

One hears over and over again, "Getting fired was the best thing that ever happened to me." People most apt to make this statement are employees who were in a bad job to begin with. While working, they denied it. But once they are out there on the street and have time to take stock of themselves, it all comes out. They hated their job. They needed to be fired.

People Who Need to Be Fired

Three types of people who seem to profit most from dismissal are the bored, the natural leader or anti-employee, and those who are in the wrong field. They are by no means the *only* types. But since they appear so often among the fired and jobless, their stories are worth studying.

The Bored

Harry Nichols, a marketing-research executive in his mid-thirties, worked in a large Park Avenue firm for ten years. Then suddenly, in six months' time, he (1) fell in love with his wife's best friend, (2) went to Tijuana for a divorce, (3) took a studio apartment in a near-slum on New York's West Side, and (4) was jilted by the best friend. During that period, he volunteered to coordinate an extremely complicated marketing plan. He did it in two days with surprising ease and was lavishly praised for it by his firm. Just before he left for Mexico, he received an inconsequential raise. When he returned, divorce papers tucked in his breast pocket, he strode into his boss's office and loudly demanded a bigger raise. He was granted a three-thousand-dollar increase. One month later, he assaulted and knocked unconscious one of his colleagues after a heated argument over the size type to be used on his presentation boards. He was immediately let go.

In an interview, Harry confided that he was not unhappy over the loss of his job. "For years, I coasted along thinking that I enjoyed working at that place. But the monotony was killing me. Sometimes I think I left my wife in an attempt to liven up things. Anyway, once I'd been through the divorce, something happened to me. All this extra drive came rushing into me. But I couldn't use it because my work was dull and too easy. I only realized it when I knocked that guy down."

William Blake once made the cryptic comment, "The fool who persists in his folly will become wise." Nothing Harry did disproves this theory. He followed his craziness to its logical conclusion and emerged fired, wise, and much less bored.

Harry was a member of middle management. Management consultant Max Hershey says that severe ennui usually doesn't strike as hard at that level: "Curiously enough, it is found most often on the highest and lowest rungs of the corporate ladder. Look deep into the eyes of the pretty receptionist whose only job requirement is keeping her desk clean and greeting people and you might see the same vacant stare in the eyes of your company president during a board meeting. Only he isn't 'bored,' he's 'weary.'" The receptionist mastered her job in two days. The president may have taken twenty years to learn his. But both know they can't go any higher and are stuck in jobs that require only ten percent of their attention. Both are clock-watchers. Both need a good kick in the ass."

Another category of people who profit from a firing is that of aggressive, independent-thinking individuals who are caught in a rigid bureaucratic company. These are the kind of people who persist in making waves and questioning authority—what Max Hershey calls "anti-employees."

The Anti-employees

James Prentiss, a talented computer programmer, was fired four times in seven years before he discovered what his problem was. Since he had great personal magnetism, he had no trouble finding new jobs. But after a few months in any organization, he would make two fatal errors: He'd amass a small, loyal army of followers (which was invariably perceived by his boss as a threat), and he would never hesitate to put his ideas or plans for the corporation ahead of his obligations to his superior.

"I always thought in terms of the corporation," he explained. "I'd say to myself, 'if this were my place, how

would I run things?' But that was not my job. My job was
to make the boss look good. And that was a different job
than the one I conceived for myself. I would probably
have gone on getting fired forever if it weren't for my wife.
She got so panicked by my erratic career, she insisted on
saving practically all my earnings. Every month, she'd dole
out a small allowance to me and stash away the rest. After
my fourth firing, she cashed in our stocks and I bought a
partnership in a small computer-programming firm. In six
months, I became its president. In four years' time, we've
nearly tripled our business. If I hadn't gotten fired, I'd never
have learned—this sounds conceited, but anyway, I'll say
it—that I wasn't made to be an employee. I was made to
run things.''

Putting up one's own shingle is an extreme solution for
the anti-employee's problems that many people simply cannot
afford. But there are some young, growing firms where the
traditional chain of command is looser and more relaxed. In
such an atmosphere, the natural leader can usually find ample
ways to express himself and stay out of trouble.

The Man in the Wrong Field

Another group that thrives on a firing are those who are
stuck in careers they should never have started. Management
consultant Harvey Christiansen says that such people hate their
jobs because they can't stop thinking that they should be doing
something else. "Other talents and skills keep welling up inside
them, begging to be exploited. Try as they will to concentrate
on their current jobs, that gnawing feeling of unfulfillment
is always plaguing them."

Lures as trivial as a friendly help-wanted ad or a cup of
coffee with a fast-talking recruiter on campus can trap people
into careers they were never meant for. Often ethnic, social,
or gender-based considerations determine into what area of
work a person will fall.

A steel-parts salesman for ten years until he was sacked for having the lowest sales graph in the company, says, "I became a salesman because my father had been one. Most people stumble into jobs for reasons like that. But when they stumble into the wrong line of work, getting fired is good for them. Look at it this way. If a man breaks an arm and it's badly set, his arm becomes malformed. In order to function again, it is necessary to go through the agony of breaking the limb again: in other words, to get fired." He is now a builder and developer in Phoenix, Arizona: "Real estate was always my true vocation."

In Peter Rauscher's case, the birth of a second child landed him in the wrong field. When he was younger, Peter wrote lyrics and music for a promising, talented singer. They were a perfect team. It was just a question of getting the public to discover them. When they were in the second year of their partnership, and engagements were scant, Peter's wife had another baby. Overwhelmed by the thought of another mouth to feed, Peter severed his partnership with the singer and took a steady job in a jingle house that serviced Madison Avenue advertising agencies.

His partner, the singer, stuck it out in the Catskills for another year until he got his first break on national television. Today he is seen so regularly his name is almost a household word. Peter, meanwhile, was still writing little ditties for soft drinks and floor wax. In spite of a nice suburban home and an occasional foray into the local musical scene, Peter was restless. In the back of his file drawer at the office, he kept a mayonnaise jar full of multicolored pills. When things got too nightmarish he'd throw down a few. Before he knew it, he was lost in daydreams of Hollywood and six-figure contracts. One day his boss got sick of looking at Peter's glassy eyes and late assignments, and Peter was a jobless jingle-writer.

"Am I delighted to have been fired? No. I've got too many financial problems. Sure, I can get another job like the one I lost. Or I can go back into show business. My ex-partner

said he'd help me out. I'm weighing every possibility. Am
I happy? Yes, I'm so goddamn happy to be out of that hole,
I don't know how to express it. And by the way, I'm off
amphetamines. Completely off,'' Peter said, one week after
he had been terminated. Eight weeks later, he got a job working
for a network show. He thinks it might be the beginning of
a comeback in his first and favored career.

These are only a few types of people with valid reasons
for being unhappy with their jobs, to whom getting fired can
be "the best thing that ever happened to them." There are
many others.

An assistant to the president of a major airline gritted his
teeth and played the patsy to his boss for fifteen years. One
sunny day in Florida when he refused to accompany the
president on a weekend boat trip, he was sacked for gross in-
efficiency. Suddenly he realized that the sycophant urge
wasn't getting him anywhere. Two months later, he became
president of a smallish West Coast airline and stopped taking his daily ten milligrams of Valium for the first time in
fifteen years.

The sales manager for a dying ethical-drug company
studied sales graphs and market-research reports every night
until he was bug-eyed. He felt if he thought hard enough, he'd
find the way for his firm to make a comeback. When the
company folded, everyone thought he was headed for a
nervous breakdown. He turned the tables on them all by
buying a tiny home-remedy plant in Ohio and marketing its
product through direct mail. He is probably a millionaire now.

An account executive, fired from his lucrative job in advertising, took his severance and invested in a Caribbean
restaurant hotel. His year-round tan is the most noticeable
effect of his career change. But he is happy to tell you that
he has also cured a bleeding ulcer, stopped biting his nails,
and is into his first successful marriage (three not-so-successful
ones having preceded this happy situation).

The people in all these case histories realized, once they were on the street, that they should correct their situations and look for different fields or positions in which they could function and find some sense of fulfillment.

There is a large group of people who unfortunately head right back into the same sort of unsuitable job they were fired from, as did James Prentiss, the anti-employee programmer in his earlier years. Like Prentiss, they may have to be fired over and over again until they see the light.

Thus far, only employees who held jobs that were injurious to them have been discussed. But there is another crew who really loved their jobs and want one exactly like it as soon as possible. It would seem unlikely that this group derives any benefit at all from the several incomeless months between jobs. Yet many formerly-fireds maintain that they gained much from their period of unemployment. Some even enjoyed it. Others say that they didn't appreciate it while it was happening, but later, in retrospect, they realized that they had somehow changed for the better.

Feeling Stronger

"Nothing bad had ever happened to me during my life. Both my parents are living. I had never been divorced and none of my children had ever been seriously ill. Then my firm went broke and I was ruined," said a mining engineer who had to remortgage his house and sell his car to keep his family eating and his house heated. "The job market was tight and I knew that it would take some time to get myself relocated. I was terrified. Every day I felt like I was going to go to pieces. But I didn't. I never cracked. After those three dreary months, I feel now that I could go through anything—the blitz, a famine, you name it."

Machiavelli wrote in *The Prince*, "There is no doubt that a prince's greatness depends on his triumphing over difficulties and opposition. Many believe that when he has the chance, an able prince should cunningly foster some opposition to himself so that by overcoming it, he can enhance his own stature.'' While it is doubtful that a person would ''cunningly foster'' his own firing, it is true that a man who has survived a firing and survived it well, is looked upon with respect.

The president of a small electronics firm stated that he'd rather hire a man who has been fired: ''I think a man who has gotten the ax once is more—how can I put it?—more *annealed*. Since he has had a little trouble, he's not apt to be irresponsible. He knows the score. Doesn't Tom Watson, the former president of IBM, seem somehow better and tougher because he was first fired from National Cash Register?''

Opening the Mind

Besides toughening a person, being ousted from the corporate world frequently opens a person's mind to new ideas and insights.

Free time and more important, a freer mind, makes people more susceptible to suggestion, more willing to try out new things and experiment with new ideas. Machiavelli wrote *The Prince* when he was exiled (read ''fired'') from the Florentine court by the Medici, and Harold Pinter turned his full attention to the theater when he was sacked as a sportscaster in London.

These are famous people. But stories of men and women who have been inspired by a firing are not limited to celebrities. Their discoveries or contributions may be on a smaller scale, but that doesn't make them any less meaningful to them.

Hank Lapham, an executive with a large cosmetics firm, said, ''While I was looking for work, I started toying around with the idea of creating new cosmetic products. For the first time in my life, I conferred with my wife about them. Here I had been living with this woman who used cosmetics every day and I had never fully considered her opinions. We continually experimented with new packaging ideas and formula combinations. By the time I was hired, I had at least five workable, original ideas in my files.''

Malory Kloester's dismissal from a Fifth Avenue retail store revealed an entirely unsuspected talent. An erratic and gifted window decorator, Malory was fired because she was a maddeningly compulsive talker. Without the slightest encouragement, she could churn out a nonstop monologue on her husband's Cardin buttons, her daily bus-rides, Chinese diplomacy—anything! It took a lot of patience and precious company time to listen.

After she was sacked, she immediately started going on interviews. Despite her considerable talent, she'd always talk herself out of a job. Soon she was going to fewer and fewer job interviews. During the empty afternoons between calls, she diverted her tremendous vocal energy to sewing together bits of leather and making belts, rings, and vests in intriguing new designs. At Christmastime, she took her leather accessories around to a few boutiques and department stores and sold them. The editor of a leading woman's fashion magazine discovered her crafts and gave her considerable free publicity. She is now contemplating opening a small factory in Mexico to help fill all her orders.

Getting fired means, for some, that for the first time they can think about business or company policies without being influenced by their former corporation's "tunnel vision." When a man is on the outside looking in, he is free to flex his intelligence, form different perspectives, and become (maybe for the first time in his life) someone who thinks for himself.

For years Marvin Redmond, a vice-president of a mammoth, now-defunct, chain of department stores, accepted the company's outdated, bureaucratic systems. When the chain went bankrupt, he was fifty-five years old and out of a job. His wife had died a year earlier of a protracted illness that had eaten up all his savings and put him severely in debt. One night, when he had nothing better to do, he jotted down on paper all the unprofitable, cumbersome procedures that eventually forced the chain to fold. After each, he noted an alternative method of handling matters. Of these alternatives, one was an imaginative and original innovation in distribution procedures. Over lunch with an executive from Sears Roebuck, Marvin sheepishly mentioned his idea. That was the end of poor Marvin's tragedies.

Artists have often recognized hardship as a means of shaking a person out of his complacency and stimulating the creative urge. Tennessee Williams, whose successes and failures are notorious, put it very eloquently in an interview with Rex Reed: "Luxury is the wolf at the door and its fangs are the vanities and conceits germinated by success. When an artist learns this, he knows where the dangers lie. Without deprivation and struggle, there is no salvation and I am just a sword cutting daisies."

The removal of luxuries does not *inevitably* jolt everyone into a new set of ideas or insights, of course. That would be too awesome. For some, being jobless simply means acquiring new experiences, but even these are often treasured highly.

Experiencing Different Things

"My life has always been very uncomplicated," said the comptroller of a small, industrial firm. "Breakfast — train — cigarettes — meetings — lunch — meetings — train — martini — kiss — bed. For twenty years, aside from the two months that I was out of work, that's how life has been Monday through Friday. "But when I was job-hunting in 1970, I had a ball. Whenever I wasn't writing letters or interviewing, I did things I'd always wanted to do but never had the time or gumption to do. I hiked. I made homemade bread — for the the first and last time.

"Going to the movies in the daytime, though, was the real

adventure. They were cheaper than going out to lunch and I saw the greatest things: old ladies in mink coats leaning on their chauffeur's arm, actors, students, beautiful housewives holding hands with their lovers. It didn't change my life or anything, but I'll never forget it." One wishes everyone could be like him and see getting fired as an opportunity to escape from routine instead of a disgrace.

When Paul Gauguin abandoned his brokerage job and went to Tahiti to paint, his admirers said he escaped. Yet when John Doe gets to sleep late, take uncrowded off-hour trains, and walk in the park and feed the pigeons for the first time in his life, he often sees himself as rejected, exiled, and dumped. Yet he is actually being reprieved—if only temporarily—from a rigidly programmed life. There are, however, some jobless souls who recognize how real their freedom is during those unemployed months. They tend to look back on it with a certain wistfulness.

An attractive photographer's assistant was out of work for six weeks during the summer in Chicago. She said, "I only had interviews about every other day and felt terribly lonely. All my friends worked and I hated sitting around my apartment. So I'd call them up and ask them to meet me in Lincoln Park for lunch. I'd have a whole beautiful picnic made with deviled eggs and cucumber sandwiches or fantastic chicken salad with water chestnuts. They'd bring a bottle of wine and we'd find a spot of clean grass and talk and look at the sky. It would drive them out of their minds to go back to work."

John Rhodes, an out-of-work fund-raiser (the same man who advises everyone to take out a bank loan the day they are fired), recalled only one noteworthy experience during his period of unemployment, but he certifies, "it changed my whole opinion of myself. I was walking down West Eighty-Fourth Street and I saw a man being held up in an alley. I swear to you that, ordinarily, I would have just walked on. But I wasn't working and I had time. I stopped and tried

to think of how I could help. The holdup guy had his back
to me. When he turned around, I did something very simple.
I tripped him with my foot. He fell and dropped his knife
and we got the stolen wallet away from him. Do you know
that one gesture—putting my big clumsy foot in that guy's
way—was one of the best things I ever did? My God, I actually
prevented a crime.''

A distinguished, white-haired stockbroker who was fired
for gambling too hard with clients' money says, ''I was fired
during the transportation strike in New York in 1966. The
streets were jammed with traffic and cabs would take up to
five passengers at a time. I'd talk to the people sharing the
cab with me. I'm a shy man—I normally never talk to strangers.
If I couldn't find a cab, I'd hitchhike. I was forty years old
and worth thirty-three thousand dollars a year and I stood
on Second Avenue with my thumb out!'' To revel in the memory of one's undignified figure is not quite the monumental
change in life that others have experienced, but maybe a
little less dignity was just what our stockbroker needed. As
Heraclitus declared, ''the mixture which is not shaken
decomposes.''

The most definitive statement about the beauty or good
side of getting fired came from Dr. Ernest Dichter, the father
of motivational research in marketing. To him, getting fired
is a dynamic, positive event, but he said, sighing, most people
would have to change their whole philosophy to agree with
him. ''Most men and women see life in static terms. They
think 'making it'—having a big house and a membership in
the country club—is their life goal. They want paradise on
earth.

''But that isn't the reason we are alive. Life's purpose is
not to experience a South Pacific type of fulfillment or to
be in the Garden of Eden any more than it's to become chairman
of the board and stop right there. It's the opposite.

''We should never be quite happy. We should always want
something new and different. Life's purpose is what I call

'constructive discontent.' That's not a terribly new thought. Goethe talks about it in *Faust* and other writings. The answer to life is continuous striving. That's the purpose: never to find. Shall I put it another way? Getting there is not half the fun. It's *all* the fun. Therefore firing is an episode that's good for you because it pushes you further.''

Dr. Dichter also said that every person in this world is capable of having three careers in a lifetime. Is it possible? A look at the obituary column in the newspaper may be the answer. Why is it that so many of the longer, more important obits tell of people who have had many job changes during their life?

On October 13, 1971, the New York *Times* reported the death of a certain Cyril Lodowic Burt. Born in 1883 in England, he did the following things in his lifetime: (1) became a classics scholar, (2) set up a child guidance clinic, (3) joined the London County Council, (4) wrote three books, (5) was an editor for a scholarly journal, and (5) became professor of education at the University of London. All this in Great Britain—the country where there is supposed to be a dearth of opportunity!

Now that he is dead, it is too late to ask Sir Cyril if he was fired out of any of his jobs or if he quit voluntarily. But it doesn't really matter. What matters is that he successfully adapted to all of his career changes and allowed himself a life of ''continuous striving,'' the description of which merited considerable space in a foreign newspaper.

The obituary column, as well as many less-celebrated formerly fired individuals, might just corroborate Dr. Dichter's view that ''firing is an episode that pushes you further.'' Certainly James Prentiss, Malory Kloester, Marvin Redmond, and others would have to agree with him. Movement and turmoil made them grow. The paradise of having a steady job didn't.

But as everyone who has been fired knows, while dismissal is pushing a person further, it is also forcing him to encounter many problems, traps, and emotional inconveniences of which those who ''see life in static terms'' (and maybe even Dr.

Dichter in his retreat in Croton-on-Hudson) are serenely unaware. This is the other side, the negative side, of the firing story.

Chapter VIII

THE NEGATIVE SIDE

David Klaus, a C.P.A. in a Cincinnati accounting firm, radiated charm and assurance. But because of the way he blatantly distorted facts and figures, his name was anathema down at the Internal Revenue Service. After five years of making excuses for him, the president of his firm decided that it was time for David to move along to another company. But David decided, No, he wouldn't go. He gave in to what is reported to be one of the fired man's most insidious temptations.

Not Letting Go

Instead of using the office space and telephone service that they had provided him for job-hunting, he continued to work on tax forms that had already been assigned to his peers. Weeks after he had been terminated, David would be seen late at night, bent over an adding machine, cheerfully working out other people's problems. The next day, he would wait until the head of the firm went out to lunch and slyly place the completed tax form on his desk.

"I wouldn't even look at the form," said the president, who was profoundly embarrassed by David's contributions. "I'd throw it out and pray he'd go away. First of all, it would be unethical for me to accept his work when I wasn't paying him. But there was more to it. I knew he was trying to get rehired and I felt cornered. He was so damn polite and humble-acting when I met him in the halls. I couldn't bring myself to fire him a second time. Finally I had the office manager take away his office space—which he really needed for job-hunting."

David was like the discarded lover who keeps coming back

with little gifts and middle-of-the-night phone calls. ("If I am generous and unselfish enough, I can control you and win you back.") It might work for lovers—especially if the other partner is subject to strong guilt-feelings—but it almost never works in business, which requires subtler psychological games. Yet people will loiter around the office months after they have been canned. Most of them don't go to the extent of handing in work, but many will stay to socialize with their peers, lean on the boss's secretary's desk, or simply wander the halls. Whether they're doing it to get rehired, make the boss feel guilty, or just wasting time, they should know that management can't stand the sight of them and that almost anywhere else is a better place to be.

The Imaginary Consultant

Second cousin to the man who hangs around the office is the imaginary consultant. This is the severed employee who *mentally* can't let go of office responsibilities and problems long after he has been evicted from the premises.

Hans, a 6' 6" giant of Dutch extraction, was the president of one of this country's largest oil companies. At fifty-six, he was firmly told to retire. The management team who had kicked him out asked their advertising agency to "hold Hans's hand for a while" and to give him "anything he wanted." One of the things Hans wanted was to continue meeting with the board of directors. So the agency obligingly organized a kind of phantom board which met once a week in a rented conference room in a mid-Manhattan hotel.

Getting together enough people who would go along with Hans's fantasies was a real challenge. All the agency could round up were Hans's stockbroker, his chauffeur, a pimp, two men from the agency, and a couple of clerks belonging to the hotel. Pounding his fist on the table, Hans would tell the motley group what was wrong with the oil industry and how he could fix it. The agency, which was footing the bill for the refreshments and yellow pads, was desperate to find Hans a job. Eventually an account executive wangled him a place on the board of a faraway Iranian oil company.

With all Hans's power and prestige, he was allowed to carry out his fantasies to their most flamboyant extremes. Other less-mighty imaginary consultants have to content themselves with calling up their ex-employees every day, filching their interoffice communications, following the company closely in the trade journals, and conducting one-way conversations at lunch on how they'd handle things if . . .

A sales representative who frequently lunches with his former and now-fired boss, was appalled by what the latter was doing to himself. "I go out with him to cheer him up and then he gets talking about the company. I hate listening to him, but I can't tell him he's making a fool of himself.

"Lots of times he's right and knows more about company problems than I do. He's got at least one hundred pounds of old memoranda in his desk at home. He told me he 'studies' them every night."

Compulsive Badmouthing

Another variation of mentally hanging-on is when the axed employee feels driven to talk against, sometimes even slander, his former corporation or boss. People who indulge in this kind of activity are clinging as hard as imaginary consultants. But they usually don't know it. Sometimes it can reach frightening proportions. A chief executive of Anglo-Saxon origin was fired from a huge radio corporation that was largely Jewish-owned. Overnight, this gentle WASP became violently anti-Semitic. At dinner parties with non-Jewish friends, he would indulge in compulsive, Hitlerian harangues on how he had been victimized by the international Jewish conspiracy and other "sheeny backstabbers." He looked very ugly. Everyone wished he would shut up.

When Lot's wife looked back, she turned to salt. People who hang on to their old job—mentally or physically—are inviting the same kind of vexing problems.

Looking Inward

Another problem is the direct opposite of that of Lot's wife. Here the fired person makes a clean-enough break with the past. But instead of picking up the pieces and marching forward, he moves inward. Lost in deep introspective reveries, he suddenly sees résumés and interviewing as so much nonsense.

Clarence Pushkin, a formerly-fired television writer, says the worst evil that can befall a man out of a job, is trying to answer the unanswerable questions. "It's those big questions —Why am I living this way? What is the meaning of life? What's the point of working?—that distract you from the job search. *Because there are no answers to those questions.* There is no rational reason why I live in Scarsdale and send my kids to good schools. I just do. And if I don't work, all that will change. I know no matter how philosophical I get, I don't want my life style to change. But the temptation to overthink my life—say after a depressing interview or when I lost out on a job—was always with me while I was unemployed."

But isn't that cowardly to avoid such deep existential problems? "When a person's employed, fine, let him be contemplative," Pushkin replied. "But if he's been fired and inundated with bills, he is too vulnerable to account for his values and former decisions. He has no real strength and can't think clearly. Later, when he has some money coming in, he can consider different life goals—because he can implement them. If he decides he wants to be a fisherman in Newfoundland, he has enough cash to buy a boat. But when he has been fired, he probably can't afford to buy a goddamn fishing rod, much less talk his family into emigrating.''

Not everyone experiences—or admits to experiencing—Pushkin's desperate kind of soul-searching. But those who do agree that it can be calamitous. ''I knew I was headed for a nervous breakdown unless I kept very tight control of my feelings,'' Pushkin continued.'' I became very rational and cut up my day just so. I devised disciplines for myself so I was constantly active and had no time to think. I shaved every morning before eight and made it a point to read the help-wanted ads in three different newspapers before ten. When I wrote a cover letter, I'd be very specific as to when I would call for an interview—so then I *had* to call.''

The Long-winded Memo

Pushkin's stoical refusal to explore the source of his discontent may seem repugnant to believers in self-analysis and other contemplative sciences. Getting to the root of one's problem, they think, is essential for mental health.

Tom Houghton ironed out his problems by writing them out. Tom, a young lawyer, was fired from a prestigious Wall Street firm for grossly neglecting an important but officious client. He hated the client and was defiantly pleased by his dismissal. But for weeks he drifted along filled with ''. . . this vague unrest. I didn't know what I wanted or what I needed. I kept asking myself what the hell difference does it make if I do anything or not. I cursed my education that had made me able to practice law. After five weeks of doing nothing, I saw an apartment that I wanted to rent but could not possibly afford. That motivated me enough to get up at five one morning and type a résumé.''

While typing, he remembered that his firm had frowned on any of its lawyers—even the younger ones—doing their own typing. It was beneath them. They were to dictate to

the secretaries or write their briefs in longhand. Now Tom
was a great two-finger typist. He hated to dictate. More than
that, he hated the imperious attitude of the switchboard
operator, who he knew was sleeping with one of the partners.
Worse, he despised the firm's policy of concealing information
for expediency's sake. And he loathed Henderson, a senior
partner who, for all his paunchy joviality, was running the
firm into the ground. One criticism followed another until
he found himself typing a memorandum to all three partners.

He vented all the bitterness and frustration he felt about
the firm. "At times I was petty and most of the memo was
cluttered with useless verbiage. But much of what I said made
sense. When a man is severed from a place, he thinks better."
By the time he had completed the document, he had (1) redis-
covered principles that he had suppressed while working for
the firm, (2) had a much better idea of what kind of outfit
he was suited for, and (3) answered most of the big questions
for himself about his life and where he wanted to be headed.

"Fortunately I let a friend of mine read the memo and
he stopped me from mailing it. Generally speaking, I don't
think a long bitchy memo should actually be sent out. They
probably wouldn't read the whole thing, and if they did, you
can imagine what kind of reference you'd get."

This doesn't mean that a long-winded memo cannot be read
by people outside the firm. If it is good enough and long
enough, it might even be sold as a book. Witness the books
written by Messrs. Culligan, Blair, Ackerman. All worked
at one time or another for the now-defunct Curtis empire (publishers of such magazines as the *Saturday Evening Post* and
the *Ladies Home Journal*). Each wrote a book about what
was wrong with Curtis. The books were actually giant memos
that told the world of their own feelings. While the general
public's interest in their books was limited, one can imagine
what salutary effects they had on their authors. They were
seeing themselves as individuals again—not just cogs in Curtis's several revolutions and ruinous undertakings. On the other

hand, Walter Hickel's *Who Owns America?* (written one year after Nixon fired him) was a real contribution to the literature of contemporary politics. Needless to say, once a memo or book has been written, its author would be wise to shelve and forget it lest he fall into the imaginary-consultant trap.

Other Cures

Instead of putting down one's grievances on paper, a few troubled and fired individuals resolve the existential-question dilemma by turning themselves inside out in front of a psychoanalyst (if they can afford it), or consulting with a priest or old friend. Still others decide the only answer to their questions is to drop out completely or change careers. Whether their answers are foolhardy or sensible, can only be known many years later.

No matter how a fired man conquers the tendency to lose himself inside himself, it's crucial that he does. For one consequence of living with unresolved problems is that a curious kind of lassitude and indifference to life can overcome him. This can be as destructive to the job search as not letting go.

Doing Nothing

"I had this feeling of depressing passivity. I didn't care what happened to me," said a chemical engineer, describing his feelings during his first two months of unemployment. "Did you ever read Kafka's *Metamorphosis?* It's about this salesman Gregor who wakes up one morning and discovers that he has turned into a giant gelatinous beetle. He just lies there on the floor of his bedroom. He can barely turn over, and his sister has to feed him rotten meat and vegetables. That's how I felt after I got fired: like an amorphous, passive, inert insect. I started to shape up when a friend told me that by sitting around all day doing nothing. I wasn't inactive at all. I was aggressively digging a hole for myself to lie in."

Max Hershey condemns doing nothing from a purely practical point of view. "If a client of mine sits watching the soaps all day or rereads the daily paper three times, it shows. I can tell he has withdrawn into himself. His responses are slower and he gets this dull, glazed-over look in his eyes. He's like a vegetable. And how am I going to get someone to hire a vegetable?"

But what is there to do in the long hours between letter-writing and interviewing? How can one throw oneself into any project when life is so precarious?

"Bicycle," suggests the chemical engineer. "It develops the leg muscles, gets you out into the fresh air, and doesn't cost anything."

"Accomplish something," says Mr. Pushkin. "Paint the house, brick by brick, very slowly."

The list of things to do is endless. Anyone can think up something. The question is deciding to.

Clinical psychologist Dr. Maurice Lemke says that no normal man really *wants* to do nothing. "He hates sitting on his ass. If he allows himself to remain inert, he is robbing himself of his will. In fact, he is behaving in a highly masochistic way. Say someone drags you to a dinner party. The food is cold and the conversation is insipid. You can hang around and suffer silently, or you can do something. This might be anything from making a quiet phone call to a friend who will call you away, to announcing that you are a practicing witch and would like to conduct a black mass.

"The person who has been fired faces a problem far graver than one who lands in a dreary party. For him to remain passive about his situation is criminal. He should never stop trying to make his day somewhat better than it was when he got up in the morning."

One of the greatest dangers of doing nothing is that a jobless individual may just wallow his way into a full-fledged identity crisis.

Identifying with Old Riley

Peter Rifkind, an insurance salesman who is now employed, happy, and secure in his new job, says that when he was fired he was totally immobilized. He could barely get out of bed in the morning and spent most of his time dragging himself around his apartment, becoming increasingly certain that he was an object of scorn to all his friends. This wasn't just theory on his part. He *knew* people were secretly sneering at him because that was how he felt about Old Riley, a former friend who was fired. For months, Riley had moped about getting shabbier and shabbier and smelling more and more of Scotch sours. Peter hated Riley and his whining and was delighted when he decided to raise poultry in the country with his sister.

For Peter to have remembered hating Old Riley and from there to have jumped to the conclusion that he was a reincarnation of his disintegrating friend was an irrational, desperate feat of the imagination. Yet certain individuals will take their firing so hard that they walk around all day feeling that the soul of an Old Riley is inhabiting their bodies. They see themselves as untouchables and imagine that everyone despises them.

Staying active might have helped Peter avoid this new person that had welled up inside him. A good look in the mirror and a little self-hypnosis (''I am not like Riley. I am aggressive, confident, peppy, and hard-working'') can also help to overcome a poor self-image, says Dr. Lemke. But Peter felt no motivation to do anything and he would have felt self-conscious droning out his virtues in an empty room.

He finally overcame his Old Riley fixation one day when he was sitting in the reception room of his employment agent.

There was a neat, confident, sober, jobless individual reading a magazine on his left. "Suddenly I realized that I was a lot more like that guy than like Riley." This kind of easy transference of what psychologists call "role models" may sound puerile to the reader. But if it restores a person's belief in himself, why not?

Looking Like Old Riley

Even if they feel like an Old Riley *inside*, most people try to hide their self-doubts and bad self-image from the public. Others, like Harrison Davies, a formerly out-of-work office administrator, revel in looking miserable. Davies developed a certain facial expression that reeked of joblessness and self-pity. Until a friend convinced Davies that he should *pretend* to be happy and confident or he'd never find a job, he went around looking like Wall Street's number one loser for three weeks. He used to sit in a park adjacent to his former office and stare into space for hours at a time. On very bad days, he'd shuffle up and down Park Row during lunch hour. His slack facial muscles, vacant eyes, and downturned mouth quickly relayed the information to everyone that he was a member of the unemployed and rapidly declining.

Why was he doing it and what was he getting out of it? "Perhaps Davies was trying to punish himself," says Dr. Lemke. "When a friend or a park attendant shook his head and felt sorry for him, he was getting the narcissistic feedback he wanted and felt that much sorrier for himself. On the other hand, he might have been trying to punish the firm that fired him—a 'look-what-you've-done-to-me' kind of ploy."

Thus far, only the fired man's conflicts with himself have been discussed. Hopefully these are his only conflicts. Unfortunately, many manage to extend their problems to include the people around them. More often than not, it's the marriage partner who gets hit first.

Conflicts at Home

"Christopher's wife left him because he got fired," was the standard explanation for a couple's recent divorce. It didn't make sense. How could she be so cruel? How could he be so dumb as to get himself into an alimony-paying situation? A little investigating proved that the breakup wasn't that simple.

Christopher's wife, Gail, left him because he had become violent and cruel with her and the children. He acted this way, he protested, because she refused to cut down expenses. She said she *did* economize. It was her husband who was extravagant. He said that she was sneering at him and that's why he had to keep up appearances—and so on *ad infinitum*. Divorce was perhaps the only way to end their arguments.

After a marriage counselor heard about Christopher's case, she said, "Those arguments never would have started if they had been intent upon supporting each other instead of tearing each other apart. We all know that a fired person needs moral support from his spouse. What is less known is that it is almost impossible to *get* support without *giving* some.

"Gail needed to be assured by Christopher that he was not crushed by the blow of being fired, that he was brave, confident, etc. Chances are Gail would have reacted well and given him all the encouragement and support he needed. By acting violent and fighting over money, he was telling her that he was scared and broken by his firing. And Gail, who must not have had much self-confidence of her own, grew frightened. And like many frightened people, she responded negatively to his weakness.

"If a person acts like he is cracking, the spouse starts worrying. It sounds callous, but the breakdown of one marriage partner (whether it's the man or the woman) is a real threat to the other. A jobless person is much better off going to a friend or some outsider to express his or her fears and self-doubts."

This doesn't mean, she explained, that a person must go

home jumping for joy because he was fired. He can be very blunt about the financial peril they are both in or about the poor job-market. He or she needs cooperation and will get it by staying cool and assuring the other that an emotional breakdown is not imminent.

"When I got fired, I painted the picture as black as I could to my wife. She's normally optimistic and I knew that was the only way to get her to economize. But I wasn't emotional about it. I just said, this is the situation, let's try to make it as bearable as possible," said a once-fired textbook editor.

"You see, I needed her help for so many things. Not just to get her to be economical, but because I wanted to hear her comments—she had a more objective view of my career. I needed to talk things over with her freely. Even small things like getting my suits back from the cleaners or reminding me to mail letters were important."

Giving Up Sex

Not going to pieces and keeping a stiff upper lip may do much to prevent tension at home. But another source of friction that frequently arises is complete sexual abstinence on the part of the fired individual. Many wives complain that their husbands won't go near them when they are out of a job, whereas a woman who is unemployed will often become as chaste as Wonder Woman. One reason for such continence, says Dr. Lemke, must date back to our old Puritan ethic.

"Although we have managed to shed much of our guilt about sex, this feeling that sex is a reward for work well-done still lingers. Successful men often feel that they need more sex than other people. You may have heard men after they've just completed a profitable business deal say, 'Now I want to go out and get laid!' Women who have risen high in their career are usually more sexually oriented in their private lives than those who have remained in inferior positions. But when these types lose a job, they begin to think they don't deserve to indulge in sex. They haven't earned the right to it. In a utopian situation, male and female prostitutes would be provided for everyone out of work," he concluded quixotically.

A bachelor news-reporter who was fired from a New York daily paper eschewed sex because "when I was out of a job, I felt that I wasn't in the running any more—like I wasn't marketable. What girl wants to go to bed with a guy who is out of a job and a potential burden? Just thinking this made me impotent."

A recently fired woman account-executive said, "I don't date at all at the moment. I'm afraid I'll break down and start clinging or leaning on the first man who is halfway decent to me. I feel too vulnerable to flirt or maintain a relationship."

It will probably be years, if ever, before most people overcome their tendency to confuse sex with economics. But it's worth the effort, says employment agent Max Hershey. "Beauty experts in fashion magazines have always recommended sex for skin, hair, and aging problems. At the risk of sounding like I am equating sex with the purchase of a Brooks Brothers suit, you've got to admit that an active satisfactory sex life is going to make a person look and act more relaxed, vital, and positive, say, during interviews, than one who feels castrated and deprived." But, he went on, giving up sex is by no means the worst thing that can happen to the fired man. "Believe me the single most subversive evil that can assault the job-seeker is plain ordinary panic."

Panic

Many people say that the ideal amount of time to be out of work is six weeks. It's longer than a vacation and gives a person enough time to alter his perspectives and enjoy his freedom. Anything longer than that (and it frequently is longer), and a friend's remark about the rotten job-market or a little needling from an in-law can get to the job-hunter. His mind goes blank, and fear takes over. That's panic.

The trouble with panic is that it usually shows. Trembling hands is one of its most common manifestations. So are keeping two cigarettes burning at once during interviews, not hearing and therefore not being able to answer questions, and forgetting what one's last sentence was.

Personnel agent Mitzi Morris says that panic is more common among older people: "Kids think that they're going to live forever. A few months out of a job doesn't bother them. They figure they can always freeload off their families or friends if things get rough. For older guys it's tougher.

"One of the worst results of panic is that it can lead a person into taking a job that's totally wrong for him. Jeffrey, a recent client of mine who is close to forty years old, was asking twenty-five thousand dollars for a job in an exciting, growing company. I found him a position in an excellent place, but they refused to pay more than twenty thousand dollars. He said he wasn't interested. I thought he was making a mistake, but I wasn't worried for him becuse I knew that eventually we'd find him the right job.

"One week went by. During that time, Jeffrey must have done a lot of thinking and talked himself into a state of panic. He called me and said he'd found a job in what I knew was a backward, stultifying outfit. And even though they were only offering eighteen thousand dollars, he'd accepted it."

If a person is prone to panic, Max Hershey suggests the following preventive measures.

(1) Make a budget and stick to it. Being broke is one of the major causes of panic.

(2) Stay away from people that put you down. Low self-esteem is the other major cause.
(3) Panic is contagious. Avoid listening to people who are themselves in its throes.
(4) Take deep breaths whenever you feel fearful.
(5) If you wake up in the middle of the night feeling panicky, don't just lie there and let your fears build. Read a book, turn on the TV—if necessary, wake up the whole house.
(6) Don't take a job until you have discussed its pros and cons with at least three people.

Probably the most comforting thought for the man who panics was contributed by an astrologist, Lionel Day: "When someone who has been fired comes to me—and you'd be surprised how many do—I say to them, what are you panicking for? You've come from a long line of people who have never starved to death, otherwise you wouldn't be here. If your ancestors survived plagues, monsoons, famines, and other acts of God, merely losing a job isn't going to do you in."

Keeping a job may, but not losing one. For unlike getting fired, its two alternatives—quitting or staying forever—can be exhausting for the average worker. However, after a hard look at the negative side of getting fired, it's possible that the subject of how never to get the ax again may be very appealing.

Chapter IX

QUITTING

"There is absolutely no inevitability as long as there is a willingness to contemplate what is happening."

MARSHALL MCLUHAN

Seeing the handwriting on the wall and quitting before the ax falls is one alternative to getting fired. As technology advances and mobility becomes more and more the new modern virtue, this judicious "job-hopping" is gaining acceptance every day.

Commenting on young executives in American industry today, writer Walter Guzzardi, Jr., declares, "The agreements between modern man and modern organizations are not like the laws of the Medes and the Persians. They were not made to stand forever. . . . The man periodically examines his own attitude toward the organization and gauges its attitude toward him. If he doesn't like what he sees, he tries to change it. If he can't change it, he moves."[1]

The problem is that there are still certain employees who have not learned to be like Guzzardi's executives. These are the people who risk getting fired. When they can't "change it," they don't move. They stay and dig their own grave.

"I should have realized my head was on the chopping block *months* before I was fired," said Christopher Soames, brand manager for a food-products concern in Chicago. "My boss put me to work on a special marketing plan that he never bothered to read. That should have been enough warning for

---

[1]Walter Guzzardi, Jr., *The Young Executives* (New York: New American Library, 1966), p. 71, as quoted by Alvin Toffler in *Future Shock* (New York: Bantam Books, 1971), p. 146.

anyone. But like a fool, I convinced myself that he was too busy to read it.''

Sam Baruch, fired as head of the new-products development of a small chemical company, said he knew a year ahead of time that his company was going to merge. He also knew that the merging conglomerate had a new-products division that was twice the size of and four times more technically advanced than his little laboratory. ''I simply didn't want to think about it because I knew I'd have to relocate to another city for another job.''

In the course of interviewing people who have been fired, most admitted that they saw some danger signs before they were sacked but did very little about them. Yet if a person never wants to be fired again, he must be able to recognize a danger for what it is and act upon it immediately (either quit, or change circumstances or performance so drastically he can insure job security).

Signs that one's job is in jeopardy fall into two obvious categories:

(1) Those that management purposefully drops to let the employee know his number is up.
(2) Those that management unconsciously or unwillingly drops that reveal that management's number is up.

When the Employee's Number Is Up

Management is rich in ways of letting a man know they want to fire him.[2] They sincerely want to prepare him for the

---

[2]These signs have nothing to do with genuine warnings whereby the boss tells his subordinate that his job is in danger if his performance does not improve. Constructive warnings of this nature are helpful to employees and rarely necessitate quitting. All danger signs discussed here have to do with cases where things are so bad that short of some cataclysmic change in the company or the employee, the latter *has* to quit.)

fatal day. "First of all, it makes the firing interview a lot easier if you've already given a guy some indication that he is not working out. He won't argue as much. And then, too, there's the outside chance that he'll quit and save us a lot of money and embarrassment," said personnel manager Everett Hardin.

On the other hand, they don't want him to be absolutely certain he's going to be dismissed. He might do something harmful to the corporation.

"It's all very complicated, this setting up a man for a firing," Hardin went on to explain. "Sometimes it has to be done very slowly. For instance, what if an executive is very well-liked by his subordinates but he is doing a lousy job? No one wants to fire a popular man abruptly. He might steal away half the staff once he gets relocated! We therefore have to subtly diminish his stature before we sack him. It kind of prepares the rest of the personnel for his departure.

"Another reason for acting slowly is that while our target is being gradually robbed of his power and prestige, we have time to train a new man for his position, to study his *modus operandi,* his files, his rapport with his associates, and his approach to his job. He's usually willing to tell us anything we want to know because he isn't certain he's on his way out or not. If he did know, he might bolt and take all our business with him or God knows—look for ways to blackmail us."

Anyone interested in quitting rather than getting fired, should be aware of the several ways management warms up an employee for a dismissal. Those most frequently reported are:

(1) *The absentia meeting.* A meeting is held about a piece of business that directly concerns the employee to be fired. He will not be invited. When he protests, he is told that he wasn't in his office when the meeting was called. The fact that the meeting was called at one o'clock, when the victim was out to lunch, should

be a clue to him that he is in trouble. A marketing analyst to whom this happened said belatedly, "My response was to stop going out to lunch. What I should have done is go on interviews during every free moment."

(2) *The absentia decision.* Akin to the above, but with one difference: In this case, the boss waits until his quarry is out of town, then makes a decision directly involving the man's department. The answer to his complaints by management: "Well, Wiggins, you were in California and we couldn't reach you." What they don't explain is that they never tried.

(3) *The office shift.* A simple way to demean a man is to shift him from a prestigious office to a lowly one. "It didn't take long for my subordinates to realize that I was going rapidly downhill when I went from a corner office to a crumby one-window dump with a desk that looked like something from the Salvation Army. Once I lost stature in my employees' eyes, I was fair game. They released me under the guise of 'bettering personnel relationships.' Baloney! They got rid of me because I had too close a look at their books," complained sales manager John Priest.

(4) *The junior jigsaw puzzle.* Here the victim's subordinates are told to report to other members of the firm on "extra assignments." This is supposedly done to give the junior staff members more experience in handling "different problems" in order to "broaden their perspectives." The only purpose of this plan is to water down the victim's authority and get his staff accustomed to working with other men in the organization.

(5) *The we-don't-know-where-you'll-fit plan.* An employee is told that there will be a reshuffling in the department, but that the total plan is not complete. "We don't know where a man of your talents will fit in this new scheme, but as soon as we do, you'll hear." That's

the last he hears of the future. As the days wear on and inertia sets in (and he looks increasingly idle and useless), he becomes easier and easier to fire.

(6) *The don't-bother-us technique.* This is a minor classic. The target is told not to bother taking his work to his boss since he knows his job so well "any supervision would be superfluous." The man to be fired may be foolish enough to think that he has finally made it in the eyes of management. While he is working in his own little department, unencumbered by direction from above, management is creating a whole new department with one subject left out. Him.

(7) *The shelved assignment.* The victim is put to work on a project and is then told that since the market situation is changed, there is no longer any use for his project. By that time, a replacement for his job has been found.

(8) *The cold shoulder.* Here the boss simply makes himself unavailable at all times to the man he wants to fire. He never is in, never stops to chat in the halls, and never answers any interoffice communication. Millionaire entrepreneur Huntington Hartford says he uses this technique exclusively. "I practically never fire anyone and hate to do it. But when I have to, I usually try to warn him by just not being available to him. I do it because I hope he'll take the hint and look for work elsewhere. That way he thinks he is quitting and a lot of animosity between us is avoided. But it's strange how some men can delude themselves into thinking I really am too busy to see them—even when a month earlier I had been around every day."

The list of techniques management uses to prepare a man for a firing could go on forever. Most of them are fairly obvious. But it is uncanny how many employees are unable to recognize their meaning and continue to nurture unproductive hopes and aspirations.

Ferreting out signs that one's own corporation is on the skids is far easier than determining one's private destiny within it. Perceiving other people's failures never seems to strain the mind as much.

When Management's Number Is Up

Clues of impending disaster come in many guises. One of the most painfully obvious was reported by an employee laid off from a now-defunct magazine. Every other week, the publishers would paste all the ad pages on a huge bulletin board in the main reception room. In 1965, the pages filled up two walls. By 1971, advertising revenue had fallen so low, the pages barely covered half a wall. "Anyone with a sense of spatial differences would have known that bankruptcy was around the corner."

Other symptoms of imminent financial ruin are too much hesitation on the part of management, an epidemic of management consultants snooping through the books, an alcoholic president or board of directors, guarded statements by management to the press that conceal everything and say nothing, and frequent changes of the palace guard.

"But it's the atmosphere that really betrays a failing company," states a former employee of a large transport company that recently filed for bankruptcy. "The offices are quieter, the phones ring less, and the secretaries take long lunch hours. Memos get petulant and meaningless. Meetings go on late into the night but nothing is resolved. But the worst is the despair you can read on your boss's face—and see reflected in your own at night."

The mystery is that if all these warnings and portents of

doom are available to the employee, why is it that so many people don't quit? Why doesn't everyone have the independence and autonomy of Guzzardi's young executives?

Why People Don't Quit

Clark Henderson, a plant manager in a chemical firm, says it's inertia—a kind of dread of change that immobilizes people. Knowing that he had defied the board once too often and that his days were numbered, Henderson described how he wrestled with the urge to leave his job.

"I'd lie awake at night and dream of going out on a limb and taking a job with a new outfit in Indiana. There were risks involved, but, I'd argue with myself, the new job was no more of a gamble than staying and maybe getting fired. It was no more financially precarious. Shouldn't a man take a chance once in a while? So what if the kids go barefoot to school? So did John Connally.

"But somehow over breakfast, I'd always come 'back to my senses.' The sound of the commuter train and seeing the kids get on the school bus made the night's craziness fade away. I'd tell myself those were just adolescent dreams to change, move, and stick my neck out. I'd convince myself that I *loved* the status quo. Chest out, stomach in, I'd stride through that plant believing that I was doing the right thing by staying and being realistic.

"And then the board of directors gave it to me when I least expected it: two weeks before Christmas. The bastards."

The standard reason most people give for not quitting is that they could not find another job. Some say they really searched. Most people, however, admit that they never looked hard enough.

Dr. Maurice Lemke has a provocative explanation for why people don't quit—or, to nitpick the question, don't look hard enough—for a new job: "When a person won't quit or look for another job even though he knows he should, he is probably the victim of two major fears: fear of failure and fear of exposure.''

Fear of Failure

"Fear of failure is a commonplace-enough fear; it's only insidious when it prevents a person from acting. Say you're going to take the California driving test. You can openly admit that you are afraid of failing because it's known to be a difficult test. But *not* to take the test, *not* to drive because you're afraid to fail is unthinkable! Muhammad Ali can't refuse a rematch because he's afraid he won't win. The whole world would know he was a coward. Yet a man who knows he should find another job won't look for one because he is afraid he'll fail!

"Since no one wants to admit his fear of failure is making him a coward, he avoids the whole question by convincing himself that he doesn't want to quit. Even though he sees his firm being gobbled up by bad debts or his career plummeting, he tells himself that moving out is unthinkable.''

Fear of Exposure

The other fear which Dr. Lemke says plagues men is fear of exposure. This is the stuff nightmares are made of.

"Most of us only know a part of ourselves—the outer part. Occasionally an experience with drugs, alcohol, or hypnosis will reveal a perverse or childish side of us we'd rather not think about. That's one of the reasons everyone would rather avoid crises or a situation that exposes him.''

On the subject of fear of exposure, Dr. Ernest Dichter did a revealing study for an airline to find why such a large proportion of our population has never flown in an airplane. During interviews with nonflying travellers, most of the people said that they did not take planes because they were afraid they would crash. Fear of dying is a respectable fear, as are all fears which involve survival. But since statistics plainly showed that flying in an airplane is far safer than getting into an automobile, this fear simply didn't make sense.

Dr. Dichter's interviewers probed further for the real, gut reason these train-riders and bus-takers didn't fly. After much questioning, it was discovered that what these people dreaded most was exposure. In other words, they were afraid that once up in the air, they would reveal themselves as nail-biting, upchucking, whimpering babies.

According to Dr. Lemke, a man who knows that he should quit, but doesn't, is suffering from the same fear of exposure. To change jobs and strike out into a void may bring to light unattractive traits he'd rather not reveal. Who knows if he'll fail further and fall farther? What if he makes an ass of himself, and his friends, wife, and children find out he's an incompetent no-talent? As long as he clings to his job—no matter how bleak his career looks—he still has some kind of protective coloring and doesn't risk exposure.

In order to shield themselves from facing their fears of failure or exposure, Dr. Lemke finds that many of his clients construct elaborate rationalizations for not wanting to quit. These rationalizations are what get him up in the morning, put him on the train, and keep him "striding through the plant." Some are preposterous. Others have a solid ring of truth. Most of them disappear at night. Their efficacy depends solely on the employee's ability to delude himself.

A little research among people who were fired (but could have quit had they really tried to find a job) bore out Dr. Lemke's observation. When asked why they didn't quit, at least half of them confessed that they had deluded themselves into thinking that they couldn't or didn't want to.

Some of the most frequently heard rationalizations for not quitting and not striking out on something new go something like this.

"I Can't Afford to Quit"

Lack of money is the reason the majority of people give for not quitting. They would lose all that profit-sharing, that stock, they'd never find a job that paid as much, or retraining would cost too much and so on. Money is also the reason why married couples who are tearing each other to pieces won't go to a marriage counselor or get a divorce and why people go to Lake Michigan ten years in a row and moan about never seeing Europe. Lack of money can be the reason for not doing almost anything.

Virginia Rider, a divorced, successful regional manager of a large furniture-manufacturing firm, makes thirty-five thousand dollars a year. Her only big expense is the support of her aged mother, a burden she shares with her two brothers. If anyone should be economically independent, she should. Yet she has no car, no stocks or savings accounts, and no real estate. And she is always two thousand dollars in debt to Checking Plus. Where does it all go?

It goes on wholesome luncheons with hefty drinks in mid-town Manhattan, impromptu dinners at home for friends with expensive wines, the hairdresser's twice a week, exquisite clothes, quickie trips to the Caribbean, and doctor bills. Since she is out sick twice a month with an indefinable illness, she has more checkups than the President of the United States. She says she loves her work. But if you catch her after a few drinks, she will tell you what she would really like to do is design her own furniture and create something more valuable "than that Grand Rapids crap I have to look at all day."

With all Virginia's money tied up in clothes and entertainment, there is no chance of her being a furniture designer and discovering whether she could make it in that field, no chance of risking exposure and failure—as long as she keeps her debts up. At the time of this writing, her firm has been nearly paralyzed by distribution problems. Things look bad. She can't afford to do anything but hang on.

"This Job Shows I Have Real Self-discipline"

Michael Loden hated his accountant job in a huge, impersonal medical insurance corporation in Chicago. He wanted to be an independent accountant with clients of his own, but was deathly afraid that he could never find enough people to trust him with their affairs. To convince himself that quitting was out of the question, he fell in love with the ideal of self-discipline.

Gritting his teeth, he drove himself with Germanic determination to perform all his despised job-duties. The more he loathed his work, the more self-discipline was required to function. And the more self-disciplined he became, the better person he was—he thought.

He became so involved with the ascetic ideal that he decided not only to be the most perfect employee, but also the most beautiful. Every day, he forced himself to get up at six in the morning, put on a track suit, run for two miles, and do fifty pushups. He didn't smoke, drink, or overeat. He had the flattest stomach of any man on his floor. But at fifty, he had such severe asthma attacks, he and his family were forced to move to Arizona. "In essence, I fired myself," he said sitting by his 40-foot pool. "I was such a good employee they couldn't possibly fire me. So my body did."

Forced to support himself in Phoenix, he rented a small office and hunted for clients with the tenacity of a bloodhound. Five years later, he is making enough money to keep two children in college at once. Judging by the way he dug into his club sandwich, the flat stomach is a forgotten aspiration.

"I Have an Impossible Dream"

People who use this rationalization yearn for an alternate career that is so unrealistic and crazy that it can never possibly be realized, thus postponing the problem of quitting indefinitely.

Hilda Ionesco, a pretty Rumanian refugee, took a job as a showroom model in 1948 when she was twenty. An intelligent, lively young woman, she found the drab atmosphere and routine of her work endlessly boring. Her dream was to go back to Rumania one day—after they had a revolution against Russian control. There was no point in attempting to start a real career in America. When she went back to Europe, she would live on her family's estate and not need to work.

The years of intolerable dullness passed—but no revolution. When Hilda was forty-five and getting a touch too plump, her boss politely told her she ought to consider another line of work. Twenty-five years of waiting for the Impossible Dream and she was unprepared to do anything but be a showroom model!

Some other Impossible Dreams frequently heard at cocktail parties: to open a hotel on a tropical island ("when I finally get some capital"), raise sheep in Australia ("after I've convinced my wife to come along"), join a commune ("but it's a pity hippies are so unsanitary"), and get into directing films ("any kind of films, just films").

"I'm So Petrified They'll Fire Me"

This more desperate, complicated rationale can submerge all emotions, and consequently the desire to quit. If a person is totally consumed by fear of getting fired, how can he act? He is in a state of total panic. Like a rabbit frozen in a car's headlights, this person can't move.

Meredith Jones, a personnel director for a Boston firm, tells this story about himself: "I'd only been in personnel work for three years when I was laid off. My company, an antiquated electrical-appliance manufacturer, could no longer afford a personnel department. I quickly found a job with a conglomerate with a reputation for running a cutthroat, turnstile operation. At first, I had some vague idea about reforming the place. It was frightening to see employees hired and fired so fast. And it was unhealthy for the company—like a dog biting its own tail.''

But every time he defended an employee or presented a plan for more reasonable personnel relations, the fishy stares he got from management put the fear of God in his heart. If everyone else was so dispensable, it stood to reason that he was too. "Little by little I sank into a totally paranoid state. My hands shook when I had to go before management. Even though I worked very hard, I was so nervous I wasn't efficient. I even started walking in my sleep at night. Living a life of fear like that, I wasn't capable of putting a résumé together, much less going on interviews.''

Meredith's anxiety reached such a point that he ended up seeing a psychotherapist. There on the couch, he discovered that: "Without knowing it, I'd been pretty traumatized by the loss of my first job (which was in no way my fault). I thought that the whole world would think that there was something basically wrong with me if I got fired again. Having two jobs in one year would make my wife think I was unstable. What would my parents say? The thought of it paralyzed me.''

Meredith was sacked after one year with the conglomerate. "But if I hadn't allowed myself to be in such a state of panic, I might have been able to find a new job before they fired me and had the dignity of quitting.''

"No Matter What I Do, It Won't Help"

In sociology and literature, there is a whole school of fatalistic, pessimistic thought that can be used to support this numbing rationalization.

Key phrases such as "other-directed," the "man in the gray flannel suit," and "quiet desperation" have become platitudes to express it. We work for a System we don't fully understand, don't love, don't especially want, and can't do anything about.

Charles Reich infused new blood into this attitude with his book *The Greening of America*. Among other indictments of the corporate state, he writes, "Jobs and occupations in the society are rigidly defined and controlled, and arranged in a hierarchy of rewards, status, and authority. An individual can move from one position to another, but he gains little freedom thereby, for in each position he is subject to conditions imposed upon it.[3]

This pessimism is an integral part of American culture says sociologist Lee Porovich. "The myth of the white-collar man as a victim of ruthless, meaningless forces stands right alongside the myth of Horatio Alger. But the former is standing two feet deep in quicksand. He's not growing, he's sinking. If he doesn't struggle or make any unexpected moves, he can just manage to keep his head above ground. But he can never get anywhere. Like T. S. Eliot's J. Alfred Prufrock, he'll measure out his life in coffee spoons." Of all the ways to smother the desire for quitting, this weary fatalism is one of the most effective. If a man has decided that it's no use, why try anything new?

Jordan O'Donahue, a former professor of psychology, joined a research firm in his mid-thirties. He was thoroughly imbued with this tragic philosophy of the business world. The crass commercialism of his clients and the way his firm manipulated statistics appalled him.

Rather than start an honest research firm of his own (a real possibility since he had inherited considerable money and small "boutique" research firms were in full flower in the sixties), he chose to stay and be society's victim. He entertained his academic colleagues and friends with tales of the venality and brutishness of the business world. Enamored of his own

[3]Charles Reich, *The Greening of America* (New York: Random House, 1970), p. 87.

eloquence, he found it much more gratifying to sit back and gripe rather than do anything about the messy morality he perceived around him.

Eventually Jordan reached forty-eight years of age. He was making thirty-five thousand dollars a year and his boss, after interviewing several less hostile young men, became aware that younger men in rival firms were doing the same work as Jordan for a salary under twenty thousand dollars a year.

Jordan took his dismissal as just another sign of management's crassness. After a year of searching for another job, he went into business for himself with two of his peers. His firm was an instant, moderate success. As if by a miracle, the world of research wasn't so brutish any more.

The above are just a few of the many rationalizations that encumber the minds of people who delude themselves into hanging on to unsuitable jobs. Other rationalizations heard in and out of the corporate state are:

"I have to sacrifice myself for the sake of my family."

"It would break my boss's heart."

"It would break my employees' hearts."

"No one else could ever run my department."

"I'm terrible at interviewing."

"I have no decent contacts."

The need for any of these rationalizations betrays trouble and discontent. Anyone who is using them, according to Dr. Lemke, would be wise to give serious thought to quitting.

That is, if he doesn't want to get fired.

Chapter X

STAYING UNTIL RETIREMENT

The other alternative to never getting fired is staying until retirement. To some the thought of remaining in a single company forever is bleak and horrifying. For them, growth means changing the scene and experiencing different challenges in different companies. But after being fired once, there may be some readers who want to settle down to one job and stick with it until they are sixty-five.

Many books on how to get ahead in business with charts, systems and intricate formulas for success have already been written. Anyone whose head is pointed in that direction is well advised to read them. This is no replacement for them. What follows here are some comments made by successful, seemingly fulfilled executives who, after being interviewed by the author on the subject of firing, turned the interview around to their own specialty: getting ahead and staying there.

All the people quoted here appeared to enjoy their work. All believed there to be enough challenge within one corporation to keep an intelligent man stimulated and happy. Charles Reich's statement that "the majority of adults in this country hate their work"[1] would bewilder them. Their opinions and advice were varied and subjective—which was to be expected. As practical-minded businessmen, they hesitated to speak from anything but experience. It is possible, however, that one or two of their trade secrets will be of use to anyone determined to keep his current position.

Picking a Department Everyone Hates

"If you want to make your mark on a corporation, find a department everyone is dissatisfied with, and then fix it,"

[1]Reich, p. 243.

suggested Frank Paulie, executive vice-president of an international petrochemical firm. "Ten years ago, I was asked to head up the shipping department. At the time we relied on independent Greek and Norwegian and other shipowners to move our oil. Because we are a large and growth-oriented company, they were screwing us right and left for transportation. The minute they knew we were in a tight market, they'd raise their freight rates. If they found out that our situation was urgent, their rates would go up even further. No one wanted the job of dealing with these shipowners. Except me.

"I knew the only way for us to hedge our shipping costs was to have *our own ships*. I've spent the last ten years fighting certain reactionary elements in this corporation to get that idea across and make it work. Today we have a large fleet of owned and chartered vessels. We've cut transportation costs to acceptable levels, and we can't be hemmed in and squeezed by our European friends."

Paulie puffed majestically on his cigar. Ten years of fighting for something he believed in hadn't only toughened him, it had made him one of the happiest businessmen in America.

"Tell people who never want to get fired to take the dog, the real dog, of a department in his company and make it work." He caressed a ship model on his desk. He was very much at home in his twenty-by-thirty office. As far as the eye could travel, there were pictures of boats, trophies, and other nautical paraphernalia.

Creating a New Department

If a dog of a department doesn't exist within one's corporation, there is always the possibility of creating a new department. An executive in the retail-food business, described how his vexation with company policy led to creating a whole new sector of business for his corporation.

"When I joined this supermarket chain, there was no gourmet department, yet we had stores in some of the wealthiest counties in the United States. Management had this stupid idea that we'd lose our fair-price image if we stocked expensive food items."

This kind of tunnel vision aggravated him so much, he fought management for two years to get them to carry a few S. S. Pierce products and a quality spice line. Eventually he convinced them to set up a gourmet corner in almost every outlet. His crusade paid off: "The gourmet line proved so successful, we're going to organize a franchise of gourmet stores in shopping centers across the country." He paused dramatically to let this information sink in, then added, "I'll co-ordinate it."

His pride in this accomplishment was impossible to disguise. His work was his life. Clearly he was a man to whom the word "escape" in travel ads would be meaningless.

Creating a New Product

By far the most effective action for the man who wants love and tenure within his corporation is to come up with a new product idea and get it marketed successfully.

Sometimes new product ideas come in a flash of inspiration. An executive with a pharmaceutical company who claims to have created the first new over-the-counter cough remedy in decades says the idea was triggered by a problem he had with his wife. When she had a cold, she refused to drink hot rum or brandy to put her to sleep. As a result, she would cough all night and keep him awake.

One day he had the brilliant idea of slipping a shot of vodka in her regular cough syrup. She stopped coughing and went out like a light; a new product—a nighttime forty-proof cough-medicine—was born.

For most people, coming up with new product ideas is hard, grueling work. Robert Casey, a New York advertising man who ran a school for copywriters during the sixties, used to tell his students that in order to create new products, they should make a list of all the things they hate about products and services currently available to them. When the list reached three pages, he made them sit down and write alternatives for them. From this exercise, a new product would almost inevitably be conceived. (For another version of how Marvin Redmond used the hate list as a creative, job-hunting ploy, see page 101.)

In *The Last Whole Earth Catalog,* a young spokesman at the Alloy Conference in New Mexico is quoted as saying, "You've got to be dissatisfied. You have to know that it's not enough. It's not giving the juice, you know? The other thing is you have to know there is a possibility."[2] Generation gap or no, there seems to be a meeting of the minds between people of all ages who want to make their mark on the world.

Focusing one's attention on problems in products and departments and then solving them is only part of the story. One must also be alert to problems within oneself. According to most of the people interviewed, the employee who is constantly scrutinizing his work—like the saint who examines his conscience nightly—is bound to get closer to paradise than the next fellow.

Assessing One's Own Work

"When I first started with this company, I decided the best way to insure job security was to ask my boss continually to appraise my work," said the young vice-president of an import-export firm who had risen to her position (over the protests of many older men in the firm) in less than five years.

"I don't mean, of course, that you should go in and say, 'Am I working out? Do you love me?' That's being a nuisance. When you want to know what management thinks of you,

[2]*The Last Whole Earth Catalog* (Portola Institute, 1971. Distributed by Random House: New York), p. 117.

ask them what they think of your operation or department. Is it growing fast enough? Are there areas in which it could function more efficiently? That makes them more objective. They'll feel freer and less embarrassed about giving you a straight story." She paused, glanced outside her office door where a seeming army of clerks were bustling about, and smiled.

"Another way to get a line on yourself is to make an unreasonable request. You could, for example, ask for three extra clerks when you only need two. Or say you want your expense account doubled. If they grant the request or at least apologize profusely for not granting it, you know you've got their confidence. If they don't, start asking youself what you're doing wrong."

Another, more independent, way to assess one's work is to compare it with the boss's. An executive in the auto industry recalls, "My personal gimmick in the early days was to keep a kind of tally sheet on my boss's and my achievements every week. My wife thought I was crazy when she saw it. But it put me where I am today. A lot of men think they are doing well if they keep a step ahead of their peers. But that's never enough. You've got to be better than your boss, so that if he is promoted or fired, there's never any question of bringing someone in from the outside to replace him. You've got to be the *obvious* replacement."

Avoiding Complacency

Hayward Stone, the treasurer of an Oregon lumber company, warns against complacency. According to him, it's the single greatest temptation the higher up the corporate ladder a man goes: "You start socializing with your superiors. You drink with them, let them cry on your shoulder occasionally, and your wives get chummy. Before you know it, you're conning yourself into thinking they really dig you for yourself. You get complacent and maybe you don't do your job as well as you used to. Suddenly you're dependent on their friendship to keep you on the payroll.''

In his view, this is the worst mistake, ''Because your boss doesn't depend on your friendship. He depends on your work. It's your work that is helping him earn his salary, that is keeping his kids in school and his pool clean and chlorinated. These things are more vital to him than you are. And if you can't cut the mustard, just see how long that friendship between you and your boss is going to last.''

Apparently he was cutting the mustard better than most. His office was larger than a one-bedroom city apartment. Asked if he had ever succumbed to complacency, he shrugged and replied, ''No, but I fired my assistant and regular golf partner a week ago. He thought he had me by the balls because he always let me win.''

Deciding to Be President

The chief executive of a large food-products firm suggests that one foolproof way to avoid complacency and keep the aggressive juices flowing is to decide to be president of one's corporation. But not by blatantly going over the boss's head or undercutting one's colleagues, he warned; that's how to get fired.

''I mean for a man to calmly decide once and for all that he is presidential material. His certitude and the fact that he has set his goals that high make sacking him unthinkable. Anyone with that much self-esteem and drive has got to be an asset to a corporation.

''The decision to be president may come very early in a man's career with nothing but blind faith to go on, or later, when he has reached the middle-management level and has proved himself to himself. Whenever the decision comes, there is no denying the exhilarating feeling it gives you—and the self-assertiveness. On the other hand, wanting to be or *dream-*

ing of being president has the reverse effect and may bring on profound and recurring depressions.'' He grinned maliciously. His exhilaration and self-assertiveness were still very much in effect long after he had arrived at the top of his firm.

Breaking the Rules

This concept is best expressed by a self-made millionaire who has spent most of his career merging unlikely companies into conglomerates, using foreign rather than American businessmen in strategic positions, and never lunching with business associates—only with his mistress of the hour.

For him the secret of success and tenure is to look for judicious ways to break with outmoded company traditions and rules. "Tell everyone who wants to get ahead to pick a trusted standard operating procedure and bust the hell out of it by coming up with a better system. Business needs independent, self-generating men who are willing to risk not thinking like the mass of corporate minds. No one is going to fire a man who has that kind of guts. A lot of sociologists claim that businessmen are totally victimized by the organization—that there's no autonomy, no chance for freedom of expression, etcetera. That's a lot of crap. They're victims of their own sheeplike mentalities,'' he thundered.

Although this kind of conscious iconoclasm worked superbly for our millionaire, there are dozens of people for whom it spells disaster. One thinks of the several young financial geniuses who flowered on Wall Street during the sixties by breaking with conventional investment procedures. Where they are now, no one seems to know. It's a dangerous, heady way to seek security. A safer, more conservative route to indispensability is to assume several different jobs within the corporation and come out knowing more about the company than anyone else.

Switching Jobs within the Corporation

The advantage of job-switching is obvious. It broadens the experience and knowledge of the employee, staves off apathy and boredom, and makes him management material way before his time.

This doesn't mean that a man should start as a salesman and suddenly ask management if he can go into administrative work—just for the sake of "getting new experience." Management—who pays for the training of its employees—tends to frown on moves that are only defined in terms of the employee's benefit.

"The key to switching," confided a master switcher who has headed up four departments in one of America's largest corporations, "is to make the switch look like something that benefits the corporation. Not you.

"The first thing the employee has to do is work his way out of his current job. He must have a man trained to replace him and be able to convince his superiors that his department will function without him. Once he has done this, he doesn't go to management and say, 'I'm free, where will I switch?' That's like wearing a big sign saying, 'I'm dispensable.'

"No, what he must do is look around for current or projected problem areas where a man will soon be needed, and say something like, 'I'm worried about our reinvestment of surplus cash. Someone ought to be in charge of that operation.'

"Since he is free and the most interested party, that someone in charge becomes *him,* and a new job is created for him. (Actually he created the job himself, but that's beside the point.) The result is that his experience is broadened and he has earned a lot of points for caring about company growth and development."

Another result of job-switching, he might have added (at least in reference to himself), is a six-figure salary and looking ten years younger than he is.

Traveling and Relocating

Like switching jobs within the corporation, traveling broadens perspectives. And since it gets the employee out from under the boss's thumb, it gives him a chance to feel more autonomous. There's also the theory that absence makes the heart grow fonder.

An employee of an international food company who spent fifteen years moving from one European plant to another before he came home to roost with a very important title and salary says, "I volunteered for a foreign assignment because the president had made me his assistant. He liked me! What could I say? But being his yes-man just wasn't my style—and it was making me unpopular with my colleagues. The only way I could tactfully get out from under the situation was to beg for a job overseas. It worked. I'm still with the firm, doing better than ever and too important to ever be the assistant to the president again."

Besides recommending travel for men who are in an untenable position at the home base, he advises it for any employee who (1) thinks he can really accomplish something away from headquarters (such as resuscitating a failing regional office), (2) has just had a divorce, (3) has never been anywhere, or (4) is bored with his current job in the company. For men starting out in a regional office, a request to be transferred to the central office is mandatory if he has his sights set on participating in top management one day.

Self-promotion

One way to keep the possibility of getting fired at bay is constantly to think up ways to promote oneself in management's eyes. Depending on one's importance and abilities, these self-aggrandizing activities can range from giving a lecture, playing golf with the head of a rival firm, volunteering to serve in the local fire department (especially if a prominent member of one's firm is also a volunteer), dating a client's daughter, inviting anyone valuable to one's career for breakfast, lunch, or dinner, organizing the stockholders' meeting, raising funds for the boss's birthday party, and buying a new suit.

"I keep a diary where I note down each week everything I did for myself and everything I did for the company. If they don't balance, I redouble my efforts on one or the other the next week," admitted one speech-giving, article-writing top executive whom management would never dare fire. What would his public say?

But then again, they might. Nothing can guarantee never getting fired. As every single executive who offered the above advice knows all too well, there's always that outside chance . . .

Concerning this possibility, the president of one of Wall Street's largest brokerage firms, whose tumultuous and erratic career is legendary, offered one consoling thought.

"Getting fired a second time is like getting your second divorce or your second operation. It's much, much easier."

AFTERWORD

When a person is fired, the last thing he wants to hear is a bunch of meaningless generalizations about his situation to "cheer him up." He wants to hear how to write a résumé, what to do with his money, how to sort out his job contacts, and how to carry off an interview. In writing this book, I have attempted to stick to these practical matters and not lapse too far into abstractions about mental attitudes or the power of positive thinking.

But this book could never be complete without including Tony Sitkin's Thought. Tony, an acquaintance of mine, was thirty-eight, had two children in private schools, a thirty-thousand-dollar mortgage, and two cars to finish paying off, when he was fired from his job as a copywriter. One week after this event, he called me up and said, "I have a thought for you to put in your book. It's about the word 'fired.' Tell people that when they are fired, they shouldn't feel rejected and trampled on. They should feel like rockets. I mean rockets are fired, right? And when they go up, they're beautiful. That's the way people should think if they ever get fired. I really believe that."

Two weeks later, he found himself a more lucrative, more interesting job than the one he had lost.

Maybe it was his mental state that did it. Maybe he was just lucky. It's impossible to say. But if the day ever comes that the words "Don't bother to come in on Monday" (or their equivalent) come shooting across a room at you, remember Tony's rockets. When they're fired, they're beautiful.